ROM 14
1 COR 8

LOOK WHAT'S MISSING

DAVID W. DANIELS

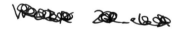

PS 25: 4 -15

IN 4: 1- 42

PS 31 :19-24

CHICK PUBLICATIONS
ONTARIO, CALIFORNIA

Published by:
CHICK PUBLICATIONS
PO Box 3500, Ontario, Calif. 91761-1019 USA
Tel: (909) 987-0771
Fax: (909) 941-8128
Web: www.chick.com
Email: postmaster@chick.com

First Printing

Printed in the United States of America

ISBN: 978-0-7589-0734-9

Foreword

Brothers and Sisters, there are two Bibles in the world. One is the real thing, straight from the apostles and prophets.

The other is not so much a new Bible, as an "un-Bible." It *removes* words, phrases and sentences. And it *adds* other words.

God condemns both corruptions. [1]

This book is specifically about what is *taken out.*

You will find out a great deal about the people who made the second "Bible" by what they took out. Mainly you will find out what they *didn't* believe.

But Satan is very subtle: he will never take out every word on a topic —only enough to confuse you concerning important doctrines, and to make you doubt what God said.

When you have a Bible changed by men, all you have are men's words. But when you have the words of God preserved in your language, you have a book like no other

---

1) See Deuteronomy 4:2; 12:32; Proverbs 30:5-6; Revelation 22:18-19

book. You have *The* Book. You no longer encounter a book —you encounter a Person.

When you see what is missing —and what is at stake— I hope you will stop trusting in the false Bible versions and trust the true and consistent Bible that has been passed down through history, which in English is known as the King James Bible.

I pray that you will become confident about what God said —and believe it.

Every word.

God bless you as you read.

TABLE OF CONTENTS

Preface: Is Your Bible Defective? 13

List of Bible Versions and their Abbreviations 15

What about the KJV Look-alikes? 18

PART ONE:
Look What's Missing—Why It Matters

1. **One Missing Word that Made Jesus a Liar** 21

2. **The Unanswered Question** 28
   The Trip of a Lifetime 29

3. **"They Took out Jesus' Words."**
   How Dare They Do That! 34

4. **The Dirty Secret about Italics,**
   Brackets and Footnotes 38
   "But it's in the Footnotes" 38
   "But it's in Italics" 39
   "But it's in Brackets" 40

5. Did God Inspire the Original Manuscripts, but Not Preserve Them? **42**

Are Copies Inspired, or only the Originals? 43

What About All Those Other Bibles? 45

6. Look What's Missing in Matthew—and Why ... **47**

7. What Do They Really Teach Your Kid in Bible College? **50**

Three Things to Watch out for 50

Want Proof? 52

One Teaching You Must Know About 53

What Does God Say about This? 55

PART TWO:
What You Should Know about the
15 Best-Known Bible Versions

8. The Root of "Modern" Bibles: ERV and ASV **58**

A Movement of Doubters 58

It All Started with Westcott and Hort 60

The English Revised Version 61

Why Was a Unitarian on the
    Revision Committee? 62

What was Different about the
English Revised Version? 64

The American Standard Version 66

What Happened after Westcott and Hort? 67

9. The Bible Becomes Ecumenical:

RSV, NRS, ESV **68**

    Can't We All Just Get Along? 68

    The Revised Standard Version 70

    How "Ecumenical" Was the RSV? 72

    The New Revised Standard Version 74

    The English Standard Version 77

    How Different is the ESV? 78

    See for Yourself 78

10. If It Looks Like a Duck...

NAS and NAU **80**

    My Story 80

    The NASB: Another Bible Built

        upon a Faulty Foundation 84

    What's Missing from the

    New American Standard? 86

    Brackets in the New American Standard 88

    The New American Standard 1995 Update 90

11. The "International" Bibles:

NIV, TNIV and NIrV **92**

    Something for Nothing? 92

    Something for Everyone? 94

    Something is Missing 95

    The Only... What? 97

    Today's NIV: a Sneaky Way to Keep a Promise .. 99

    What's Missing from the TNIV? 101

    New International Reader's Version (NIrV) ... 102

    What's Missing from the NIrV? 102

12. Error Paraphrased:
LB and NLT **104**
　More Good Intentions... with the
　　Same Faulty Foundation 104
　What's Missing from the Living Bible? 106
　The New Living Translation 106
　What's Missing from the
　New Living Translation? 107

13. The "Pick and Choose Bible:"
AMP (The Amplified Bible) **108**
　The Verse That Would Not End 108
　The Reader That Becomes the Bible Translator . 109
　Those Irritating Italics 111
　What's Missing from the Amplified Bible? ... 112
　Do We Need a "Multiple-Choice" Bible? 113

14. A Counterfeit Message: (MSG) **114**
　The Problem with Paraphrases 114
　Getting Creative with the Truth 116
　Is The Message a Bible? 119
　What's Missing from The Message? 121

15. The Bible that Almost Was: CSB **124**
　A Third Foundation 124
　The So-Called "Majority Text" 126
　The Faulty Foundation for the CSB 128
　What's Missing from the
　Holman Christian Standard? 129

16. How Much Scripture Are We Allowed to Doubt? .. **133**

PART THREE:

What's Missing from Your Bible?

17. Look What's Missing... in 40 Versions **137**

The Short List: 45 Missing Verses
in Modern Bibles 137

The Big List: 257 Verses Missing Text
in Modern Bibles 146

Missing Titles of the Lord Jesus Christ **146**

What's Missing? "Lord" 147

What's Missing? "Jesus" 153

What's Missing? "Christ" 157

What's Missing? "Jesus Christ" or
"Christ Jesus" 168

What's Missing? "Lord Jesus Christ" 169

Missing Words Concerning the Godhead ... **170**

What's Missing? The Godhead
(Father, Son and Holy Ghost) 171

What's Missing "God" 172

What's Missing? "The Father" (of the
Lord Jesus Christ) 175

What's Missing? Only "Begotten" Son 177

What's Missing? Mary's "Firstborn" Son .. 180

What's Missing? "The Son of God" 180

What's Missing? The Eternal Son 181

What's Missing? Only "God" is "good" ... 182

The Holy Spirit and man's spirit 183

**Missing Words Concerning the
Gospel Message** 185

What's Missing? Belief in Christ
for Salvation 185

What's Missing? Christ Died "for us" 186

What's Missing? Christ Alone Shed
His "blood" to Pay for our Sins 187

What's Missing? Christ's Blood
of the "New" Testament 188

What's Missing? We are Not
Saved by Works or Riches 188

What's Missing? Repentance 189

What's Missing? Details of Christ's Mission . 190

What's Missing? Other Gospel Doctrines 193

**Missing Words Concerning Salvation
and Damnation** 194

What's Missing? Words Regarding Hell ... 194

What's Missing? Words Regarding
the Second Coming 195

What's Missing? Words Regarding
the Resurrection of the Dead 196

What's Missing? Words Regarding the
Judgment and Eternal Punishment 197

**Missing Words Concerning
Heaven and Angels** 199

What's Missing? Words
Concerning Heaven 199

What's Missing? Words about the
Doctrine of Angels 201

• Angels of God 201
• Satan 203

**Missing Words Concerning
Prayer and Fasting** 203
Other Missing Words of Christ 205

**Missing Historical Details Concerning the
Life of Christ and the Early Church** 214
What's Missing? Details from
the Life of Christ 214
What's Missing? Details of
the Early Church 226

Missing Doctrines of the Apostles 228
What's Missing? Adultery 228
What's Missing? Fornication 229
What's Missing? Other Words God
Wrote Through the Apostles and Early
Church Leaders 229

18. What's Missing—at a Glance 240
Chart A: Alphabetical Order by Version 240
Chart B: In Order of the Number
of Verses Affected 242
Chart C: In Order of Date of Publication 243

Afterword 245

Index of Scriptures 247

Index by Bible Version 251

PREFACE

Is Your Bible defective?

If your Bible is not a King James Bible, it is probably missing words, phrases, and even verses. And these words, phrases and verses are important.

How important?

And how can you know for sure whether your Bible is defective?

That's what this book will show you.

In Part One you will see how important it is that your Bible shows you every single word of God, translated correctly into your language. Your Bible is seriously flawed when those words are missing. They are no longer the words of *God*. They are only the words of *men*.

You will see how many of the newer Bibles have sneaky little notes that actually place doubt in what God said.

Then you will learn what is *really* taught to your pastors, teachers and your children in Bible College. You will see for yourself why those students come out *less* sure of God's words and *more* filled with doubt.

Many people have begun to see the errors in the NIV. But not only the NIV has errors. So Part Two will give you a quick overview of 15 of the best-known Bible versions, with a small sampling of what is missing in each of them.

Part Three is a select list of 257 verses. It will show you which of those 40 Bible versions are missing important words, phrases and verses. You will be shocked.

The point is simple. When you find out for yourself what is missing, and what is at stake, you will be ready and able to discern which Bible is God's words, and which are the devil's clever counterfeits.

I pray you will, as I do, place your trust, not in man's opinions, but in the exact words of the Living God in English, the King James Bible.

You can stake your eternal destiny on it.

LIST OF BIBLE VERSIONS AND THEIR ABBREVIATIONS

Below is a list of every Bible version covered in this book, along with its abbreviation: [2]

- KJV = King James Bible (1611)
- AMP = Amplified Bible (1954-87)
- ASV = American Standard Version (1901 – American revision of the ERV)
- Bar = The New Testament: A New Translation (1968, 69, William Barclay)
- BBE = Bible in Basic English (1949, 64)
- CEV = Contemporary English Version (1995)
- CJB = Complete Jewish Bible (1998, David Stern)
- CSB = Holman Christian Standard Bible (2001, 04)
- DBY = Darby Bible (1884, 90)

---

2) Please note: most modern Bible versions are changed every couple of years, so it is impossible to know whether the newest copy will still be missing all these words. But it is very likely that most, if not all of them will, because they are based upon the defective Alexandrian texts. Every effort has been made to pick verses that have *not* changed through Bible editions.

- • DRA = Douay-Rheims (1899 – Roman Catholic)
- • ERV = English Revised Version (1881, 85, Westcott and Hort) THE ONE THAT STARTED THE TROUBLE
- • ESV = English Standard Version (2001)
- • GNB = Good News Bible (1992, American Bible Society)
- • GWN = God's Word to the Nations (1995)
- • HNV = Hebrew Names Version of the WEB (ongoing as of 2009, Public Domain, based on the ASV)
- • ICB = International Children's Bible (1986, 88, 89 – from the NCV)
- • ISV = International Standard Version (1996-2009, Bible almost complete as of early 2009)
- • JB = Jerusalem Bible (1967 – Roman Catholic)
- • LB = Living Bible (1971)
- • MOF = The Bible, a New Translation (1950, James Moffatt)
- • MRC = Messianic Renewed Covenant (2003-04)
- • MSG = The Message (2002)
- • NAB = New American Bible (1970, 86, 91 – Roman Catholic)
- • NAS = New American Standard (1963-77)
- • NAU = Updated NAS (1995)
- • NCV = New Century Version (1987, 88, 91)
- • NEB = New English Bible (1961, 70)
- • NET = New English Translation (2004)
- • NIrV = New International Readers Version (1995, 96, 98)
- • NIV = New International Version (1973, 78)
- • NJB = New Jerusalem Bible (1985 – Roman Catholic)
- • NLT = New Living Translation (2004)
- • NRS = New Revised Standard (1989, National Council of Churches)

- • NWT = New World Translation (2006 online version – Jehovah's Witness)
  - • Phi = New Testament in Modern English (1958, 59, 60, 72, JB Phillips)
  - • REB = Revised English Bible (1989)
- • RSV = Revised Standard Version (1946, 52)
  - • TCW = The Clear Word (2003)
- • TNIV = Today's New International Version (2001, 05)
  - • WEB = World English Bible (ongoing as of 2009, Public Domain, based on the ASV)
  - • WNT = Weymouth New Testament (1912)

WHAT ABOUT THE
KJV LOOK-ALIKES?

Bibles that look like the KJV[3] are not covered in this book. Here's why.

This book is about a single topic: words intentionally removed from the Bible. This is a horrible reality, and it reduces the words of God to the words of men. But it is only half of the equation.

The other important topic is what is *changed*. Words mean specific things. And all through history, words have held those meanings, both in their original languages and through God-anointed translations. But beginning in the late 1800s, modern "scholars" have *changed* the meanings of words into what the Lord never meant.

They changed God's words into what they think God *should* have said.

All the Bible versions that are missing God's words also changed the meanings of God's words.

---

3) KJV look-alikes include the New King James, American King James, Modern King James, etc. Usually they have "King James" somewhere in the title.

But many "King James look-alike" Bibles also fall into that trap. Bibles like the New King James Version used a Greek and Hebrew text pretty much like the King James, but they changed the meanings of words to match those corrupt Bibles listed in this book.

Almost all modern Bibles[4] have changed the meanings of God's words. But that is a totally different topic. This book focuses on what is *missing* from God's words.

---

4) The only exceptions are some "KJV Look-alike versions" that will be dealt with in another book.

PART ONE

LOOK WHAT'S MISSING —
WHY IT MATTERS

1

ONE MISSING WORD THAT MADE JESUS A LIAR

NUM 23:19

God is no liar. Remember these words:

> God is not a man, that he should lie; neither the son of man, that he should repent: hath he said, and shall he not do it? or hath he spoken, and shall he not make it good?[5]

When God says He will do —or not do— something, you can be sure He will keep His word. So if a Bible changes something to make God look like a liar – *watch out!*

That is not from God —period.

Believe it or not, some Bibles and perverted Greek texts actually turn our Lord and Saviour, Jesus Christ, into a liar. See for yourself in the following story.

5) Numbers 23:19.

JN 7:1

❧   ❧   ❧

The Lord Jesus had just spent the last few months in Galilee. The Jewish leaders wanted Him dead —as fast as possible. [6] The Lord knew it. But Jesus is God. *He* chose the time and the place of His death, not man.

1 PT 1:18-20
REV 13:8

Yes, He was going to die at Jerusalem, but not until the exact moment He had known since the foundation of the earth. [7] So He ministered in Galilee and avoided Judea. But things were about to change.

Now the Jews' feast of tabernacles was at hand. [8] *JN 7:2*

Each year, every single Jewish male was required to attend three feasts in Jerusalem: Unleavened Bread (the 7 days that began with the Passover feast), Pentecost (50 days after Passover) and Tabernacles (around September-October). They were known as the *Shalosh Regalim* (Three Pilgrimage Festivals). [9] *2 CHRON 8:13*   *MT 13:55*

Jesus' half-brothers [10] James, Joses, Simon and Judas, [11] were packed and ready to leave. The caravan was already moving down the road. (These "early birds" wanted to get a good room before they were all filled up.) You can almost hear them calling out: "Come on, let's go."

Then they saw Jesus.

Why wasn't He packed? He wasn't going to stay home

---

6) See John 7:1.
7) See 1 Peter 1:18-20 and Revelation 13:8.
8) John 7:2
9) See 2 Chronicles 8:13.
10) Same mother, but their father was Joseph, not God the Father.
11) See Matthew 13:55. God later used James and Judas (Jude) to write two books of the Bible.

during a required feast, was He? That wasn't like Him. That "goody two-shoes" never acted like everyone else in the family. He *never* broke a rule. JN 7:5

It was like Moses was living in their house. They didn't believe in Him[12] and were probably a little jealous of all the attention He got. So they did what many siblings do: they mocked their big brother. James, the next oldest, probably did most of the talking:

> …Depart hence, and go into Judaea, that thy disciples also may see the works that thou doest.[13] JN 7:3

Were they encouraging Jesus? Not hardly. Jesus' entire hometown of Nazareth had lost out on seeing any big miracles in their midst because of their *unbelief*.[14] MT 13:58 MK 6:5-6

So the brothers hadn't seen Jesus' miracles either. They had only heard stories about them… and they had their doubts. (Don't let the brothers' "holy speech" fool you.)

They continued:

> For there is no man that doeth any thing in secret, and he himself seeketh to be known openly. If thou do these things, shew thyself to the world.[15] JN 7:4

They were basically saying, "You can't be a public figure and hide in secret, Jesus," sarcasm dripping from their every word. "If You are able to do miracles, show the world."

"*If* thou do these things?"

12) See John 7:5.
13) John 7:3.
14) See Matthew 13:58 and Mark 6:5-6.
15) John 7:4.

Their words echoed the words used by the Tempter:

> If thou be the Son of God, command that these stones be made bread…[16]

> If thou be the Son of God, cast thyself down…[17]

What could Jesus do? It looked like He had two options:

Option A: Stay in Galilee and break the Law of Moses.

Option B: Go on out in public and possibly get killed by the Jewish leaders.

Which would Jesus choose? According to some Bibles, this is what happened next:

> You go up to the feast. I am **not** going up to this feast, for my time has not yet fully come. After saying this, he remained in Galilee.[18]

This Bible version says Jesus chose option A: to stay in Galilee and for the first time in His life, break the Jewish law that He Himself had given to Moses. But wait. The story is not over. Look at the next verse:

> But after his brothers had gone up to the feast, then **he also went up**, not publicly but in private.[19]

So according to this Bible version, He didn't break the Law of Moses after all. He just *lied to* His brothers about what He planned to do.

Do you understand the doubt this Bible version creates?

---

16) See Matthew 4:3 and Luke 4:3.
17) See Matthew 4:6 and Luke 4:9.
18) John 7:8-9, English Standard Version.
19) John 7:10, ESV.

[Handwritten margin notes: MT 4:3, 6 / LK 4:6, 9; JN 7:8-10 ESV NOT KJV!; JESUS LIED? ACCORDING TO ESV, YES!]

First it says the Lord Jesus told his brothers he was *not* going to the feast. So his brothers thought He was going to break the Law of Moses intentionally. That's a crime against God.

They would have gone down to Jerusalem thinking, "Jesus broke the Law"? They would never again feel the same about Him. Now they would object whenever anyone called him "blameless" or "sinless." They could say, "Jesus broke the Law. It was all a lie."

If *this* Bible version were true, that's what they would have thought all the way up to Jerusalem. But that's not all.

One day at the feast, they would have looked over and seen Jesus. He sneaked down into Jerusalem.

"Okay," they would have thought, "so He didn't break the Law of Moses after all. Instead, Jesus just *lied* to us, His own brothers." DANG!.

How would they ever believe Him again?

His own brothers would never believe Him when He said that He was "the way, the truth, and the life." [20] JN 14:6

The Bible says clearly that God *never* lies. But this Bible makes it look like Jesus lied. So does this Bible falsely imply that Jesus is not God? That's what it says.

Ouch.

Do you see the trouble this defective Bible makes? The lies it pushes? How can you even call this a Bible?

Don't worry. It's not the *real* Bible. This Bible depended on an ancient manuscript that was headed for the fireplace.

---

20) See John 14:6.

That manuscript was so messed-up that it was "corrected" by up to 10 different people over the years, until they gave up on it and finally abandoned it in a desert monastery.[21]

Yes, the translators of this Bible put their faith in a piece of trash and changed their Bible version to match it.

That Bible also depended on the Roman Catholic Latin Vulgate.

And do you know what caused all this confusion? One missing English word, three letters: y—e—t.[22]

Look again at that crucial verse in a *complete* Bible:

> Go ye up unto this feast: I go not up *yet* unto this feast; for my time is not yet full come.[23]

That is completely different. Now it makes perfect sense. Jesus wasn't going to go with His brethren, but He still intended to go. He just went in His own timing, away from the crowds, almost in secret. The next two verses back that up perfectly:

> When he had said these words unto them, he abode still in Galilee. But when his brethren were gone up, then went he also up unto the feast, not openly, but as it were in secret.[24]

Oh, what a huge difference one little word makes. I don't know about you, but I could never trust a Bible that

JN 7:8-10 KJV

---

21) See *Answers to Your Bible Version Questions* (2003), pp. 145-155, "Can you prove the perverted Sinaiticus was found in a wastebasket?" Available from Chick Publications.
22) In Greek, it's three letters, too. They took away *two letters* and added *one* letter. The difference between the truth and the lie is the difference between "oupō" (not *yet*) and "ouk" (not): *just three letters.*
23) John 7:8 (KJV).
24) John 7:9-10 (KJV).

is based on flawed manuscripts and makes the Lord Jesus into a liar.

The following English Bibles are all missing that little word "yet" from John 7:8:

- ASV
- CEV
- DBY
- DRA
- ESV
- GNB
- JB

- MOF
- MRC
- NAB
- NAS
- NAU
- NEB
- NET

- NJB
- NLT
- NRS
- REB
- RSV
- TNIV

That's a lot of Bibles. And they cannot be the perfect words of God. They are the imperfect words of man.

But brace yourself. We're just getting started.

2

THE UNANSWERED QUESTION

PROV 16:1 [handwritten]

> The preparations of the heart in man, and the answer of the tongue, is from the LORD. [25]

Does your church practice infant baptism? Probably not. Why not?

There is only *one* verse in the whole Bible that tells what must happen before someone can be baptized. But did you know that a lot of Bibles simply leave that verse out?

Your pastor may have been trained on the King James Bible, so he knows it's supposed to be there. His mind may even "fill in the blanks" when he reads the passage from a Bible that leaves it out.

But what about all the young people in the congregation who were not brought up on the King James?

UH OH! [handwritten]

---

25) Proverbs 16:1

They might never know that this verse belongs there. And worse, they might believe all those "textual notes" that say it doesn't belong, and end up deceived about this doctrine which is vital to Christian growth. UH OH!

Read the following story and see whether you think this missing verse is important.

THE TRIP OF A LIFETIME

He had just seen Jerusalem, the priests, and even the Temple itself... but only from a distance. He was bewildered. "How could I be so close, and yet so far away?"

EX 20:10

The Jews called him *Ger Sha`ar*, a "proselyte of the gate."[26] He kept the ceremonial law, but he was neither baptized nor circumcised as a Jew. It was impossible —because he was a eunuch.

As the treasurer for Queen Candace of Ethiopia, he had just started the long trek back from Jerusalem. But in his visit, there had been "stop signs" all along the way.

He had worshiped God —but couldn't do it in the Temple. He had offered burnt offerings —but no other sacrifices were allowed. He had listened to teachers —but none would come near a eunuch. (This was their way of obeying the Torah, you see.[27] DEUT 23:1

So there he had stood, in the Court of the Gentiles, unable to take another step toward the God of Israel. But from one thing he was not hindered: reading the holy scriptures.

On his trip home, the Ethiopian took the long des-

---

26) This term comes from "thy stranger which is within thy gates" from Exodus 20:10.
27) They based their action on this verse: "He that is wounded in the stones, or hath his privy member cut off, shall not enter into the congregation of the LORD" (Deuteronomy 23:1).

ert road south toward Gaza, avoiding the path that would put him near civilization. He needed time to think, to read God's holy words.

"If only someone could answer my questions," he thought as he again attempted to understand the Hebrew scroll of Isaiah that he had purchased at great price from scribes in Jerusalem.

Little did he know God was about to act.

Earlier that day, God sent the angel of the Lord to Philip, telling him to take that same desert road in the middle of nowhere. So he walked along, wondering what God could have in store for him.

Soon his question was answered. A caravan passed by and the Spirit of God said, "Go near, and join thyself to this chariot." So he ran up to it. And what did he hear? Isaiah 53. Praise God.

He asked quickly: "Understandest what thou readest?"

The eunuch answered, "How can I, except some man should guide me?"[28] ACTS 8:30-31

The eunuch wanted Philip to come up and sit with him in his chariot.

And he did. This Jew was different. While the eunuch marveled, Philip sat down right next to him and opened up the scriptures, preparing to read about the "Suffering Servant." Listen to the eunuch's question:

> I pray thee, of whom speaketh the prophet
> this? of himself, or of some other man?

---

28) Acts 8:30-31

Acts 8:35

Philip's answer was simple. He "preached unto him Jesus."[29] Jesus is the one the prophet was writing about.

One question answered.

As Philip preached, he gave to him the whole counsel of God. Why not? They had a long journey ahead of them.

MT 28:18-20

Suddenly, as the eunuch heard the commands of the resurrected Lord,[30] he shuddered. Oh no! Baptism? But as a "proselyte of the gate" I'm not permitted to be baptized. Was this another "stop sign"? He wanted a personal relationship with the Lord God, just like the Jewish people had —but now *this!*

This was the most important question of his life. He had to ask it. Then he saw his chance: an oasis appeared almost out of nowhere. He summoned up his courage and asked the question that filled his heart.

> See, here is water; what doth hinder me to be baptized?

Then what happened?

The eunuch stopped the chariot, Philip baptized him and suddenly disappeared. The End.

• • •

"Wait a minute!" I hear you say. *"That's all?* What was the answer to his question?" Well, if you have a modern Bible version, that's all you have. Verse 37 is missing. There **is** no answer to the eunuch's question.[31]

---

29) Acts 8:35
30) See Matthew 28:18-20.
31) Some might say, "Wait —it's in *my* Bible, in brackets, italics, or a footnote." That doesn't count. Read Chapter 4 to learn the *dirty secret* about those notes.

But if you have the King James Bible, God's preserved words in English, you know the answer from the next verse:

> And Philip said, If thou believest with all thine heart, thou mayest. And he answered and said, I believe that Jesus Christ is the Son of God.[32] ACTS 8:37

The answer to his question was simple and direct: Believe in the Lord Jesus Christ, the Son of God, with all your heart. And upon his confession of faith he was baptized.

Since his work there was done, God zapped Philip 70 miles away to Azotus, before the baptismal waters even cleared from the eunuch's eyes.

So why is this whole verse, Acts 8:37, missing from so many versions? Because from the moment the "institutional church" got the idea to baptize babies, they had to choose: either obey the scripture and stop baptizing babies, or dump the scripture and keep their tradition.

You see, this is the *only* verse in the Bible that says you must believe before you can be baptized. Babies aren't old enough to believe, so they don't qualify. This verse forces you to pick one: the tradition or the scripture.

Unbelievably, instead of dumping their man-made doctrine, they took away the verse.

Problem solved? Not quite. God was clear.

> Ye shall not add unto the word which I command you, neither shall ye diminish ought from it...[33] DEUT 4:2

---

32) Acts 8:37
33) Deuteronomy 4:2

Revelation 22:18-19 is even more emphatic about what God thinks of those who add to or take away from His words. Yet millions of Bibles read by over a billion people do not contain this vital verse —Acts 8:37.

ༀ   ༀ   ༀ

Here are some of the English Bibles that are missing Acts 8:37:

- Bar
- BBE
- CEV
- CJB
- DBY
- ERV
- ESV
- GNB
- GWN
- HNV
- ICB
- JB
- MOF
- MSG
- NAB
- NCV
- NEB
- NET
- NIrV
- NIV
- NJB
- NLT
- NRS
- NWT
- Phi
- REB
- RSV
- TNIV
- WNT

Was a Bible *you* like in that list? Don't be fooled. If it's missing that important verse, ask yourself: what else is missing?

3

"THEY TOOK OUT JESUS' WORDS." HOW DARE THEY DO THAT!

> For whosoever shall be ashamed of me and
> of my words, of him shall the Son of man be
> ashamed, when he shall come in his own glo-
> ry, and in his Father's, and of the holy angels. [34]

My friend read the verse, but he couldn't believe his eyes. He set down the KJV and again picked up the NIV I had handed him earlier. He stared at it. He turned it over. Then he examined the spine.

"Are you sure this is a *complete* Bible?"

He stared at it and my King James Bible again. "They took out Jesus' words." He was dumbfounded.

I'm just like you. When I find out something that is really interesting, I have to share it with someone. So when

_____
34) Luke 9:26.

I learned that my friend Mike, a serious Bible-believer, was using an NIV, I just had to show him some important words of Jesus that some enterprising "scholars" decided to leave out.

Were those words important? Let's find out.

ഇ   ഇ   ഇ

There had been a sudden change in Jesus' ministry. Everyone saw it. For three years He had preached the gospel and healed the sick throughout Israel. But now His demeanor changed. There was a new note of determination about the Lord Jesus.

LUKE 9:51

He stedfastly set his face to go to Jerusalem.[35]

It was normal for Jewish people to travel to Jerusalem for the Feast of Tabernacles. It was also typical behavior to avoid Samaria like the plague. Why? Because the Samaritans were not pure Jews. They were a mixed race.

Yet Samaria was located right in the middle of the Holy Land. To avoid it, pilgrims had to go miles out of their way, crossing over to the east side of the Jordan river north of Samaria and crossing back on the south side. Jews by definition did not want to step on Samaritan land.[36] Yet that is exactly what Jesus started to do.

They came to "a village of the Samaritans," and Jesus sent messengers ahead of Him to ask permission to enter in and find lodging. But when they understood Jesus was heading for Jerusalem, they flatly refused Him.[37]

Lk 9:52-53

---

35) Luke 9:51
36) The scriptures state simply, "...for the Jews have no dealings with the Samaritans" (John 4:9) For their history, see 2 Kings 17:24-41; 24:10-16; and 25:8-12.
37) Luke 9:52-53

This got two of His disciples very angry. Here was the prophesied Messiah of Israel, the Promised One, coming to their town, and they didn't even have the decency to let Him lodge there for one night?

The nerve of these people. James and John felt righteous anger against those Samaritans. —Or so they thought. They strode up to Jesus and asked:

> Lord, wilt thou that we command fire to come
> down from heaven, and consume them, even
> as Elias [Elijah] did? [38] *Lk 9:54*
> *2Ki 1:10-14*

Hadn't James and John been listening to the words of Jesus for the last three years? Didn't they understand His plan? [39] These guys totally missed the point of Jesus' coming. If they ever needed the Lord to straighten them out, it was now. *Lk 9:44; Mt 17:22; Mk 9:31*

So what did Jesus say? If you have an NIV or many other Bibles, you'll never find out.

> But Jesus turned and rebuked them, and they
> went to another village. [40] *Lk 9:55B-56*

What a letdown. Don't you wish you knew what Jesus said to them? Don't you wish you had His words to them right in your hand?

If you have a King James Bible, you do.

> But he turned, and rebuked them, and said,
> Ye know not what manner of spirit ye are of.
> For the Son of man is not come to destroy

---

38) Luke 9:54. See 2 Kings 1:10-14.
39) He had just taught them about His betrayal and murder. See Luke 9:44; Matthew 17:22; and Mark 9:31.
40) Luke 9:55b-56 (NIV).

men's lives, but to save them. And they went to another village. [41]

Wow! Such a powerful statement. Jesus didn't come to *destroy* these people. He came to *save* them. Jesus' reply is why this story is in the Bible. Remove those words and the story has no punch line, no conclusion, no reason to be in the Bible.

And yet, that is exactly what modern Bibles do.

Those are some of Jesus' most important words on this earth. But with most modern Bibles, you would never even know He said them.

These English Bibles are missing Luke 9:55b-56:

- ASV
- Bar
- BBE
- CEV
- CJB
- CSB
- ERV
- ESV
- GNB
- GWN
- CSB

- ICB
- ISV
- JB
- LB
- MSG
- MOF
- NAB
- NCV
- NEB
- NET
- NIrV

- NIV
- NJB
- NLT
- NRS
- NWT
- Phi
- REB
- RSV
- TNIV
- WNT

Brothers and sisters, it matters what is missing.

---

41) Luke 9:55b-56 (KJV).

4

THE DIRTY SECRET ABOUT ITALICS, BRACKETS AND FOOTNOTES

For there is nothing covered, that shall not be revealed; neither hid, that shall not be known. [42]

"BUT IT'S IN THE FOOTNOTES"

Ask yourself: When you look at a footnote, do you think to yourself "God wrote this"? Or do you realize that it's only man's opinions?

Seriously, if God *really* wrote those words, what are they doing in the footnotes? They should be in the main text. So if there are any extra Bible words in the footnotes, we already assume they're not the words of God. And when

---

42) Luke 12:2

they are important words, like the ones I have been showing you, being stuck in the footnotes makes you doubt them, not believe them.

On top of that, many Bibles are "basic text editions." That means there are little or no footnotes in them. So, even if God's words were placed in the footnotes, many people would never read them. Besides, how many people read footnotes, anyway?

But there is one thing we should always read in a Bible version... *the Introduction.*

When we pick up a Bible version, the first thing we want to do is look up old familiar verses and see what special notes and other "extras" are included.

But to understand a modern Bible, there is something much more basic we need to do: read the Introduction. That is where we find out the true meaning of the italics, brackets and footnotes. They have different meanings in different Bibles. Don't guess. Be sure.

"BUT IT'S IN ITALICS"

Italics mean different things, depending upon the Bible version. In the King James, they are usually a simple way to tell that the words are not *literally* in the Hebrew or the Greek, but are needed to make sense in English.[43] What do they mean in other Bibles?

In the Introduction to the *Amplified Bible* we learn that italics point out:

1. Certain *familiar passages* now recognized

---

43) For the one exception to this general rule, see *Answers to Your Bible Version Questions* (2003), pp. 120-122. Available from Chick Publications.

AMP BIBLE TRANSLATORS ITALICIZE WORDS BC THEY BELIEVE AREN'T PART OF SCRIPTURE!

as *not adequately supported by the original manuscripts.* This is the primary use of italics in the New Testament, so that, upon encountering italics, the reader is alerted to a matter of textual readings...[44]

Did you see what they said? Italics are mostly there as an excuse to put in words that "are familiar" to Christians (mostly from reading the King James Bible). But the translators don't believe those words.

But if they don't believe them, why don't they simply remove them?

Because, Brothers and Sisters, if you saw all that was missing because they didn't believe it, you'd think twice about buying their Bible. So they act like hypocrites and put it in the Bible text anyway, even though they don't believe it belongs. It's weird how they are willing to lie like that.

And what do they mean by "the original manuscripts"? We will deal with that in a bit.

"BUT IT'S IN BRACKETS"

Brackets vary in shape and number in modern Bibles. But they are most often either single [ ] or double [[ ]]. They are not used in the text of the King James Bible. But you often find them in other versions.

Here is the definition found in the New American Standard (NAS) and NAS 1995 Update (words vary slightly between editions):

---

44) From *The Amplified Bible* (Zondervan Publishing House: Grand Rapids, Michigan, 1987), Introduction, p. viii. Emphasis mine.

[ ] Brackets in the text are around words probably not in the *original writings*. [45]

The Holman Christian Standard Bible put it this way:

In a few places in the NT, large square brackets indicate texts that the HCSB translation team and most biblical scholars today believe were not part of the *original text.* However, these texts have been retained in brackets in the HCSB because of their undeniable antiquity and their value for tradition and the history of NT interpretation in the church. [46]

Did you notice that both of these introductions mentioned "the original manuscripts?" Why are they so important? Read the next chapter and find out.

ॐ   ॐ   ॐ

The Amplified Bible is also missing that important word "yet" from John 7:8 (see Chapter 1) because they put it in the text, but in brackets.

The following Bibles are also missing Acts 8:37 (see Chapter 2), because they put it in the text, but in brackets or italics:

• *AMP* • *ASV* • [CSB] • *ISV* • *MRC* • [NAS] • [NAU]

The following Bibles are also missing Luke 9:55b-56 (see Chapter 3), because they put it in the text, but in brackets or italics:

• *AMP* • *DBY* • *MRC* • [NAS] • [NAU]

---

45) This example comes from *The Ryrie Study Bible,* New American Standard Translation (1976, 78), p. xi. Emphasis mine.
46) The *CSB Red-Letter Text Edition Bible* (2004), p. ix. Emphasis mine.

5

DID GOD INSPIRE THE ORIGINAL MANUSCRIPTS, BUT NOT PRESERVE THEM?

MT 24:35; MK 13:31; LK 21:33

Heaven and earth shall pass away, but my words shall not pass away.[47]

It's hard to find a Bible introduction that doesn't mention "the original" texts, manuscripts or autographs. What are they? Are they important?

The first time a person writes something, that is the "original autograph."

So when a Bible writer first penned what God put in his heart, that writing was the original autograph of that book. Everything else is a copy.

Now if we had those originals stored somewhere, they

---

47) These are *Jesus' own words*. See Matthew 24:35; Mark 13:31 & Luke 21:33.

would be the end of all arguments about what the "autographs" said. But godly people lovingly used those originals so much that they eventually disintegrated from the weather and constant use. Thank God He put it on people's hearts to copy and translate those words.[48]

ARE COPIES INSPIRED, OR ONLY THE ORIGINALS?

2 TIM 3:16-17

> All scripture is given by inspiration of God, and is profitable for doctrine, for reproof, for correction, for instruction in righteousness: That the man of God may be perfect, throughly furnished unto all good works.[49]

All scripture is inspired, but what does the Bible call "scripture"? Why, *copies* of the originals, of course. In the verse above, Paul wrote to Timothy that all scripture was given by God's inspiration. But take a look at the verse before that, at what he said about what qualifies as "the holy scriptures:"

> And that from a child thou hast known the holy **scriptures**, which are able to make thee wise unto salvation through faith which is in Christ Jesus.[50]

3:15

Did Timothy or his synagogue have the originals? No. He had copies of copies of copies. Then, is God saying through Paul that perfect copies are scripture?

Exactly.

---

48) For more about the original autographs, see the simple illustrations in *Did the Catholic Church Give Us the Bible?* (2005), pp. 10-18. Available from Chick Publications.
49) 2 Timothy 3:16-17. Emphasis mine.
50) 2 Timothy 3:15. Emphasis mine.

Jesus read from a *copy* of a scroll of Isaiah in His hometown synagogue in Nazareth. When He finished reading, the first words He said were:

> This day is this scripture fulfilled in your ears.[51] Lk 4:21

Jesus is the one who gave these words to Isaiah. So if there was a single word out of place, He would know it. But Jesus didn't correct *one syllable* of the words He read. And more importantly, look at what the Lord Jesus called it: *scripture.*[52]

So the copy Jesus read from, and the copy that Timothy learned from, were just as much "scripture" as the originals given through the apostles and prophets.

God doesn't want us running on a wild goose chase in the desert, trying to find the "originals." He wants us to look for exact copies and accurate translations of those copies of His inspired words. Those are "the scripture."

So when you are looking for the preserved copies of scripture —the ones that Jesus said "shall not pass away"— what are you looking for?

Do you believe God's preserved words are a mishmash of writings that disagree with each other, lower or question the Godhood of Jesus Christ, and leave the reader in doubt of basic Christian doctrine? Believe it or not, that is what some people are looking for.[53]

Or are you looking for a Bible that believes Jesus is ab-

---

51) See Luke 4:21.
52) For an easy, 5-lesson Bible study on what God says about the scriptures, see *Why the King James Bible Is the Perfect Word of God* by Gary Miller (2006). Available from Chick Publications.
53) You will find out more about them in Chapter 7.

solutely 100% God and 100% man, is clear and consistent on basic doctrines, and lifts up your faith? God did keep His promise and preserved those words all the way through history. In English, we call it the King James Bible.

> The words of the LORD are pure words: as silver tried in a furnace of earth, purified seven times. Thou shalt keep them, O LORD, thou shalt **preserve them** from this generation **for ever.**[54]   PS 12:6-7

And *anything* that takes away from those words, which God promised to preserve, is not the word of God, no matter how many times it claims to follow "the original autographs."

Look through history at God's faithful and persecuted people. The King James matches their Bible.

WHAT ABOUT ALL THOSE OTHER BIBLES?

These other, "modern" Bibles are not from this preserved line. They come from picking and choosing words from corrupt Bibles made in Alexandria, Egypt.

The writers there *didn't* believe Jesus is God. They thought they were smarter than everyone else. So they were not afraid to remove important words, phrases and verses found in the preserved Bible.[55]

Know what happened to these Alexandrian manuscripts? The Roman Catholics used them as the founda-

---

54) Psalm 12:6-7, KJV. Emphasis mine.
55) But even then those Alexandrian "scholars" could not agree among themselves. See *Answers to Your Bible Version Questions* (2003), pp. 15-18. Available from Chick Publications.

tion for *their* Bible. Then they spent nine centuries hunting down the real Bible to destroy it. But faithful Christians protected it —even with their blood.

When the "scholars" behind modern Bible versions claim they are following the "original manuscripts," they are really referring to those Alexandrian manuscripts.

But God promised to preserve only one Bible, not two. There is only one Bible you can stake your faith on.

That Bible is the King James Bible. AMEN!

6

LOOK WHAT'S MISSING IN MATTHEW —AND WHY

Most of us know the familiar saying:

> Red sky at morning, sailors take warning;
> Red sky at night, sailors' delight.

In most places, that saying usually holds true. But in hotter, drier climates, it doesn't always work. So people in those climates (if they don't want to look silly) don't repeat that familiar saying there.

That's exactly what happened in Ancient Egypt.

Those self-styled "scholars," like Origen and his gang in Alexandria, came upon this well-known scripture, Matthew 16:2-3:

> He answered and said unto them, When it is evening, ye say, It will be fair weather: for the sky is red. And in the morning, It will be foul

weather to day: for the sky is red and lowring [threatening a storm][56] O ye hypocrites, ye can discern the face of the sky; but can ye not discern the signs of the times?

Origen must have thought, "It hardly rains here, even when the morning sky is red." So he did what any self-respecting Alexandrian "Bible scholar" would do. He took it out of his Bible.

The other Alexandrian "scholars" must have thought the same thing because they took it out of their Bibles, too. No harm done. It's just a little scripture. Right? *Wrong*. But don't worry; God had Bible-believers all over the earth who kept it in, right where it belongs.

But that put modern Bible translators in a bind. You see, they were taught that the best Bibles in the world[57] were from Alexandria, Egypt. Yet it was obvious their "best Bibles" were horribly flawed here.

What would they do? Would they remove all 32 Greek words, like their favorite Egyptian texts (which everybody would notice and maybe not buy their "new" Bible)? Or would they put them back in, even though it proved them to be hypocrites? Hmm

They thought and thought. Finally they put back in 31 of those 32 Greek words. To this day in their "modern" translations, only that one Greek word is missing. Know what it is? It translates into three familiar English words:

---

56) For simple definitions of less-familiar words, see *The King James Bible Companion* (2006). Available from Chick Publications.
57) Their favorites were these two: Sinaiticus and Vaticanus. When those two agreed on anything, they were told, that was supposed to be the "original Greek."

BUT THEY ALWAYS DISAGREED W/EACH OTHER

O ye hypocrites.

Isn't it ironic? Those three words reveal just what they are: hypocrites, because they ignored their own supposedly "best Bibles" and took out only what they themselves didn't want.

Brothers and sisters, you can tell a lot about ancient and modern Bible "scholars" by what is missing from their Bibles.

These English Bibles kept Matthew 16:2b-3, but are still missing those three words, "O ye hypocrites":

• AMP	• GNB	• NET
• ASV	• GWN	• NIrV
• Bar	• ICB	• NIV
• BBE	• ISV	• NJB
• CEV	• LB	• NLT
• CJB	• MRC	• NRS
• CSB	• MSG	• NWT
• DBY	• NAB	• RSV
• DRA	• NAS	• TCW
• ERV	• NAU	• WNT
• ESV	• NCV	

The following English Bibles simply deleted all 32 words, from Matthew 16:2b-3:

• MOF • NEB • REB

The Amplified Bible is also missing all 32 words, because they put it in the text in italics; however they removed that one offensive Greek word. DANG!

Now it's time to learn what your kid is *really* taught in Bible college.

7

What Do They Really Teach Your Kid in Bible College?

And he [Jesus] did not many mighty works there because of their unbelief.[58] MT 13:58

THREE THINGS TO WATCH OUT FOR

Most Christians think they are sending their child to a "conservative" Christian college. But you need be aware of what most Bible professors (and some pastors) are teaching your kids.

Your professor may say this:

"God's words *were* inspired, back when He gave them to men to write down."

---

58) Matthew 13:58.

If he does, then you need to ask him if he believes what God said about *preserving* His words. Read and think about these verses for yourself:

> The words of the LORD are pure words: as silver tried in a furnace of earth, purified seven times. Thou shalt keep them, O LORD, thou shalt preserve them from this generation for ever.[59] *PS 12:6-7*

Matthew 24:35, Mark 13:31 and Luke 21:33 (Jesus' own words):

> Heaven and earth shall pass away, but my words shall not pass away.

If Jesus' words shall not pass away, that means they exist. We can find them.

If the professor believes these words, then he must believe that God has preserved His Bible somewhere. The only issue, then, is where we can find them. That is a good start. It is based upon faith.

But your professor may say this:

"Only the *original manuscripts* were inspired."[60] *WHAT?!*

If he does, that should raise up some big red flags.

ROM 1:17; 5:1-2 Our Christian life is based upon faith in God.[61] We trust God to keep His word. When God says He will preserve His words, we must trust Him to keep that promise.

---

59) Psalm 12:6-7: Make sure you read these words in a King James Bible. Modern versions have changed the words and taken away this clear promise of God.
60) Gleason L. Archer, Jr., in *A Survey of Old Testament Introduction* (Chicago: Moody Press, 1964, revised 1974), p. 24, said "But what about the text of the Bible as we now possess it? ... It would take nothing short of a miracle to insure the inerrancy of a single copy of an original manuscript."
61) See Romans 1:17; 5:1-2.

But if your professor does not trust God to keep His promises, don't trust your professor.

Sooner or later, that doubting professor will start questioning the words in your Bible (if you use the KJV) in class. If he starts saying that certain words, phrases, or verses don't belong in the text, or if he talks about the "best manuscripts from Alexandria," he will be showing his true colors.

You see, eventually, anybody teaching about Bible versions or ancient Bible manuscripts will trust a text from one of two cities: Antioch of Syria, or Alexandria, Egypt.

If you follow the trail from Antioch of Syria, you will end up with the King James Bible, God's preserved words in English.

If you follow the trail from Alexandria, Egypt, you wind up with hundreds of Greek texts and English translations that will never agree with each other.

WANT PROOF?

Chapter 17 lists 257 Bible verses, comparing missing words, phrases and even whole verses among 40 different Bible versions. All of these are "Alexandrian-influenced" Bibles. All of them claim to use the "most reliable Greek Text" to decide what to take away from God's words. But almost none of them agree as to which words to remove.

Following that chapter are simple charts that summarize the results. Get some Bible versions out and check those verses for yourself.

If your professor lifts up your faith in God's preserved words, praise God.

But if your professor tries to make you doubt God's words, even using the results of the "science of textual criticism," *watch out!* The Devil himself delights in getting us to doubt God and His words.[62] MT 4:6-7, LK 4:9-12

ONE TEACHING YOU MUST KNOW ABOUT

One college student after another has fallen from his or her faith, simply from believing the results found by the supposed "science of textual criticism." So what *is* the "science of textual criticism?"

Textual criticism is doubt disguised as "science."

> Now the serpent was more subtil than any beast of the field which the LORD God had made. And he said unto the woman, Yea, hath God said...[63] GEN 3:1

What is the secret of "textual criticism"?

One of the earliest modern Bible critics was a guy named Johann Albrecht Bengel (1687-1752). He made his own edition of the Greek New Testament. He also made up his own rule for figuring out what to put in or leave out of the Bible. And every "textual critic" has built his house of cards upon that basic rule:

"Proclivi scriptioni praestat ardua"

(That means, "The harder reading is to be preferred.")

So if the reading doesn't make sense, contradicts other Bible verses, calls into question basic doctrines or lowers the deity of Christ, it is to be preferred. In other words,

62) See Matthew 4:6-7 and Luke 4:9-12 for one example.
63) Genesis 3:1.

they are looking for a contradictory and inconsistent Bible. And they found it: right there in Alexandria, Egypt.

Want proof? Here are the two main rules (or "canons") of textual criticism:

• *The External Canon*: "Manuscripts are to be weighed and not counted." This means if almost all the manuscripts in the world say *one* thing, and the textual critic's favorite manuscript says *another* thing, then he would give more "weight" to his favorite (usually from Alexandria) than a stack of consistent Bible texts.

But wait —God promised to preserve His words.

• *The Internal Canon*: "That reading is best which explains the others." This means if the textual critic can make up some kind of "family tree" to explain his favorite reading and convince others, then he would call his favorite reading "best."

That's not science. It's more like "science falsely so called," as God had Paul write to Timothy:

> O Timothy, keep that which is committed to thy trust, avoiding profane and vain babblings, and oppositions of science falsely so-called... *LIKE EVOLUTION?*

Where does the "science of textual criticism" lead? Let's let a couple of textual critics speak for themselves.

Kirsopp Lake (1872-1946)

After a lifetime of research and study, and after being professor of early Christian Literature of Harvard University from 1914-1938, Kirsopp Lake wrote these words:

In spite of the claims of Westcott and Hort
and of Von Soden, we do not know the original form of the Gospels, and *it is quite likely
that we never shall.*[64] HOW DID HE GET A JOB
TEACHING AT HARVARD?!

Frederick Cornwallis Conybeare (1856-1924)

This guy had impressive credentials: Fellow of the British Academy; Fellow and Praelector (Lecturer) at University College, Oxford; and Doctor of Theology. In his *History
of New Testament Criticism,* he lifted his nose high against
Bible believers, saying:

> …the ultimate [New Testament] text, if there
> ever was one that deserves to be so called, is
> *for ever irrecoverable.*[65] EDUCATED FOOL!

Textual criticism is not an act of faith. It is an exercise
in doubt and leads only to despair.

WHAT DOES GOD SAY
ABOUT THIS?

God had Peter write these words:

> For we have not followed cunningly devised
> fables, when we made known unto you the
> power and coming of our Lord Jesus Christ,
> but were eyewitnesses of his majesty.[66] 2 PT 1:16

In a similar way God inspired John to write:

> That which was from the beginning, which

---

64) *Family 13 (the Ferrar Group): The Text According to Mark with a Collation of
Codex 28 of the Gospels* by Kirsopp Lake, Silva Tipple Lake and Silva Lake (Chris-
tophers, 1965), p. vii. He originally wrote these words in 1941. Emphasis mine.
65) *History of New Testament Criticism* by FC Conybeare, (NY: G.P. Putnam's
Sons, the Knickerbocker Press, 1910), p. 168. Emphasis mine.
66) 2 Peter 1:16.

we have heard, which we have seen with our eyes, which we have looked upon, and our hands have handled, of the Word of life; (For the life was manifested, and we have seen it, and bear witness, and shew unto you that eternal life, which was with the Father, and was manifested unto us;) That which we have seen and heard declare we unto you, that ye also may have fellowship with us: and truly our fellowship is with the Father, and with his Son Jesus Christ.[67] I JN 1:1-3

It's not that evidence makes textual critics not believe. But their disbelief leads them to create false evidence.

And that false evidence, that "science falsely so called," is the "science of textual criticism."

Know what's missing among textual critics? Their faith.

They slap on the name "science" when they don't want you to question them anymore. But I encourage you: question everything they say.

As you read chapter 17, keep in mind two big questions:

1. Are these missing words important?

2. Why would someone take these words out of the Bible?

Remember, you can learn a lot about someone by what he removes from his Bible.

67) 1 John 1:1-3.

PART TWO

WHAT YOU SHOULD KNOW
ABOUT THE 15 BEST-KNOWN
BIBLE VERSIONS

8

THE ROOT OF "MODERN" BIBLES

English Revised Version (ERV) ᵁᴷ.
American Standard Version (ASV) ᵁˢᴬ

A MOVEMENT OF DOUBTERS

Today we are living in the midst of an unprecedented movement of Bible-doubters. Satan keeps trying his hardest to destroy faith in the Bible in the hearts of Christian people.

And he finally found a strategy that worked.   GEN
3:1-5

How does he do this? By pushing the lie that "the Bible has to be fixed" and whispering "Yea, hath God said?"[68] pretending there's something wrong with the Bible every time they don't understand a Bible verse.

I just read a commentary by a famous Bible scholar. He

---

68) See Genesis 3:1-5.

didn't understand how one verse followed another. But he was too proud to say, "I don't understand how this goes, but this is what I think it means." So what did he do? He blamed the Bible, saying the verse "is probably affected by the *corrupt text*."[69]

Without a shred of evidence, he made up the idea that the text was corrupt, rather than believe he didn't understand what God said.

There are many Bible verses I have not understood. But that did not make God or His Bible wrong. I simply did not understand them. Think about it —it makes no sense to doubt God and His words just because we don't understand them. It is our understanding that is to blame, not God.

Do you see what is happening? Satan wants you to doubt the Bible —God's own words that He preserved for you. The Devil has worked systematically, creating a leadership of Bible *dis*believers, trying to infect your own church, and destroy your own faith.[70]

It isn't hard to find Bible *dis*believers. Many of them are teaching right now in our Bible colleges and seminaries. The history of Bible *dis*belief goes all the way back to the Garden of Eden.

But we don't have to go that far to find the root of the modern "text critical" movement and modern Bibles. Let's just go back to the mid-1800s and a pair of scoundrels named Westcott and Hort.

---

69) See *Notes on the Bible* by Albert Barnes (lived 1798-1870) at Proverbs 7:23. Emphasis mine.
70) See *Did the Catholic Church Give Us the Bible* (2005), pp. 130-137. Available from Chick Publications.

IT ALL STARTED WITH
WESTCOTT AND HORT

If you read certain books today, you would think two angels named Westcott and Hort descended from heaven to hand us a "better" Bible, kind of like the way Joseph Smith claimed to receive the Book of Mormon and Muhammad claimed to receive the Qur'an.

But nothing could be further from the truth.

After the littlest smattering of New Testament Greek, Fenton John Anthony Hort was quickly led by his buddy Brooke Foss Westcott to books favoring "Biblical criticism"[71] and using the perverted Greek texts of Roman Catholic JMA Scholz, of Constantin Tischendorf and others.

But before he did his own research, Hort had to make a decision: would he trust his doubting teachers and so-called "text-critical scholars," or would he believe his Bible?

Believe it or not, he chose to dump his Bible and believe his teachers. Do you see what he did? He dropped the complete, preserved words of God and bought into the doctrinally perverted Bibles of Origen and others, who didn't even believe Jesus Christ was God Almighty.

The effect was almost immediate. Within weeks Hort ignorantly slandered the preserved Greek text, and libelously wrote, calling it "...that vile *Textus Receptus*...."[72]

---

71) Biblical criticism seeks to treat the Bible as "any other man-made book." It uses men's made-up theories about how the Bible evolved into its present form. They refuse to believe what God clearly said in the scriptures. But as Christians, God honors us when we have faith in Him, not when we doubt Him. (See 2 Timothy 3:15-16; Hebrews 11:6.)

72) Hort himself admits this in one of his letters. See *Life and Letters of Fenton John Anthony Hort,* edited by Arthur Fenton Hort (New York: Macmillan & Co., 1896), Vol. 1, p. 211. Available for free download on www.books.google.com.

Westcott and Hort were brainwashed by their professors into doubting the Bible almost as soon as they began working with the "critical" Greek New Testaments.

Two years later, they devised a plan to secretly create a "new" Greek text from which to make a "new" English Bible to replace the King James. But it *wasn't* new. They simply cut out words they didn't want[73] and pasted in whatever their favorite Alexandrian Greek texts said.[74]

So their Greek text took out hundreds of words, phrases, even whole verses that God had preserved through Bible believers over almost 2,000 years.

What kind of "scholarship" is that?

And these two guys are the "fathers" of the modern Bibles? Think carefully. If you cannot trust the method they used, you will not be able to trust the Bible they created, either.

THE ENGLISH REVISED VERSION (1881)

For 19 years Hort and Westcott worked on their scheme to make a "new" Greek text. Their goal was for everyone to throw away the preserved Greek text behind the King James Bible and grab hold of the "new" one they created by picking and choosing their favorite readings out of the Alexandrian stream of manuscripts.

In 1870, as they worked toward completion of their

---

73) Of course, that wasn't easy, because unlike the preserved words of God, the Alexandrian texts don't agree with each other in hundreds of places. So they made up their own arbitrary rules to decide *which* contradictory "reading" they would stick into their "new" Bible.
74) Their favorites were two huge Alexandrian Bibles (or *codices*) called the Sinaiticus and the Vaticanus.

Greek text, they were offered the opportunity to be on the "Revision Committee" to rewrite the KJV. At last. This was their chance to change the English New Testament to match their made-up Greek. And they mostly succeeded.[75]

In 1881 they released their own Greek text, complete with its own theory of textual criticism in book form.[76] The next week they released the English Revised Version New Testament.

It was quite a package deal: they sold the public a vastly changed Bible with scores of important words, phrases and verses missing, and backed it up with their own "new" Greek text and introduction book to textual criticism.

WHY WAS A UNITARIAN ON THE REVISION COMMITTEE?

Unitarians do not believe Jesus is who He says He is: the only begotten Son of God, and Himself the everlasting God, just as much as His Father. A Unitarian also refuses to believe that God the Father, God the Son and God the Holy Ghost are together the one eternal God.

Alexandrians didn't believe in Jesus' eternality and divinity, either. Their "scholars" and scribes chipped away words from important verses that talked about the Lord Jesus being God. As they did, they cut out one of the most important verses on the Godhead from their Bibles: 1 John 5:7.

---

75) Most of their preferred readings were used by the ERV and ASV Bibles. But Bibles made since then are almost identical to Westcott and Hort's perverted text.
76) This was released in 1882 as *The New Testament in the Original Greek: The Text Revised* by Brooke Foss Westcott D.D. and Fenton John Anthony Hort D.D., Introduction & Appendix (Cambridge: Cambridge University Press). Available on www.books.google.com.

This is nothing but sinful, wishful thinking on their part. You see, if Jesus wasn't really God Almighty, they wouldn't have to take His words so seriously or believe His clearly stated promise to preserve His words.[77] Then they could change or reinterpret the scriptures however they wanted, whatever made them happy in their sin.

This is what they did. And brothers and sisters, this was exactly what God said they would do:

> Professing themselves to be wise, they be-
> came fools, and changed the glory of the un-
> corruptible God into an image made like to
> corruptible man....[78] ROM 1:22-23

So are you really surprised that Hort insisted that his English Revised Version committee have a Unitarian on board? Hort actually complained about:

> … the moral damage that would have been
> done to the acceptance of the Revision by the
> laity [non-ministers] if Unitarians had been
> outlawed as such[79]

Hort also thrilled over:

> …the weight of acceptance won beforehand
> for the Revision by the single fact of our wel-
> coming an Unitarian....[80]

Look at these two comments carefully. It wouldn't be

77) See Matthew 24:35; Mark 13:31; Luke 21:33; Psalm 12:6-7 (KJV) and Revelation 22:18-19.
78) Romans 1:22-23
79) To Westcott on August 1st, 1870. See *Life & Letters of Fenton John Anthony Hort* (London: Macmillan and Co., 1896), Vol. 2, p. 140. Available on www.books.google.com.
80) To Dr. Lightfoot (another Reviser) on September 1st, 1870. See *Life & Letters*, Vol. 2, p. 140.

"moral damage" to keep Christ-denying Unitarians out of the Revision Committee. It was their Christian duty.

And wait a minute: how did the Revised Version win "acceptance" even before it was written? Hort said it was because of their "welcoming an Unitarian." But why would scholars like a Bible better if one translator rejected the Trinity and Christ's eternal Godhood?

That's easy. Because some of the heretics who created the whole "false science of Biblical criticism," that rejected God's preserved words, were themselves Unitarians.(81)

Doesn't that make you suspicious about what those Bible Revisers really believed? It sure woke me up.

WHAT WAS DIFFERENT ABOUT THE ENGLISH REVISED VERSION?

Look what the ERV started:

It was the first major English Bible to destroy "the mystery of godliness" in 1 Timothy 3:16 by removing "God" at the right spot. The real Bible states that "*God* was manifest in the flesh." But the Alexandrian and Roman Catholic Bibles remove God and say "*who* was manifested in the flesh." By removing one word they removed the Godhood of Christ out of the verse.

The ERV was the first major English Bible to remove 1 John 5:7, taking away the Godhead. By removing those words, they removed the unity of the Father, the Word (the Lord Jesus Christ) and the Holy Ghost as one God.

[Margin note, handwritten: DENIED THE TRINITY AND CHRIST'S DEITY!]

---

81) Some of these Unitarian authors were Daniel Mace (a Presbyterian preacher) in 1729, Gilbert Wakefield in 1791, Thomas Belsham in 1808, Abner Kneeland in 1823, John Gorham Palfrey in 1828, Samuel Sharpe in 1840, and George R. Noyes in 1869.

The ERV was the first major English Bible to remove Acts 8:37, the only verse that says one must believe before one can be baptized. (See Chapter 3.)

The ERV sneakily changed 2 Timothy 3:16 from the clear and understandable "*All scripture is* given by inspiration of God, and is profitable..." to "*Every scripture inspired of God is* also profitable..."

What did the Revisers mean by that? *Only* those scriptures they accepted as "inspired" were profitable. They saw all the rest, like the Kings, Chronicles, other historical writings and even the Prophets, as written by "good men," but not inspired by God. [82]

This is just one of many examples of doctrines changed by a single word. [83]

Out of the scripture selections in Chapter 17, the ERV is missing 217 important words, phrases and whole verses that God carefully preserved. So the ERV became the "hole in the dam," opening a flood of corrupt bibles that was about to burst upon the Protestant and Baptist world. DANG!

The ERV was a set-up from the beginning. Three friends, Westcott, Hort and Lightfoot, agreed in advance on what they wanted. [84] Then they pushed the others to accept it.

Carefully, page by page, Westcott and Hort submitted their Alexandrian Greek readings on pieces of paper to the

[Handwritten margin note: GIVEN BY GOD'S INSPIRATION, ALL SCRIPTS DENIED ALL SCRIPTS]

---

82) For instance, see how Hort himself claimed a prophet of the Bible is a man speaking on behalf of God, leaning on his perception of "all that is going on around him... coloured by the events, the thoughts, and the feelings of his own time, which take hold on his own heart" —not someone relying on the exact words given to him by the Living God. See *Village Sermons* (London: MacMillan and Co., 1897), pp. 209-210. Available on www.books.google.com.

83) Many more examples of what is changed will be listed in an upcoming book.

84) See *Life and Letters of Brooke Foss Westcott* (1903), Vol. 1, pp. 389-393.

Revision Committee. And they used their reputation as Greek scholars to get the others to vote on using *their* readings and reject God's historically preserved words. Westcott even sulked when he didn't get what he wanted:

> Westcott's friend "Bishop Ellicott, who sat on the Revision Committee, recalled how Westcott—when one of his renderings was rejected—would retire with a look of solemn resignation on his face—as if his life-work had been destroyed at a stroke. When the Revision Company was equally divided on some nice point of translation, Westcott always found it difficult to vote on either side; generally he preferred to withdraw to a corner of the room until the vote had been taken."[85]

In the end, Satan made sure that enough of Hort and Westcott's text got in that it was no longer God's preserved words —just man's opinions.

The ERV was a "critical success." That means it didn't sell well, except among "Bible critics." But that didn't matter. The damage was done. The English Revised Version (ERV) became the root of the "modern" English Bibles.

THE AMERICAN STANDARD VERSION
(1901)

The Revision actually had two committees, not just one. Both English and American Committees worked on the counterfeit Bible. They disagreed on quite a number of issues. But they agreed on one thing: each group would

---

85) See *Bishop Westcott* by Joseph Clayton (London: A.R. Mobray & Co. Limited, 1906), p. 74. Available on www.books.google.com.

get a turn at putting together a Bible version for its country. The English Revised Version was printed by Oxford and Cambridge presses in two parts, the New Testament in 1881 and the whole Bible in 1885.

In the ERV the main American objections were usually printed in the back of each Testament. But in 1901 the Americans got their turn. Their version was printed by Thomas Nelson & Sons[86] and became known as the American Standard Version (ASV).

The ASV was also a "critical success." (You guessed it. Only the "Bible critics" and a few liberal churches loved it.) But it became the root of many "new" American Bibles.

WHAT HAPPENED AFTER WESTCOTT AND HORT?

After the deaths of Hort (1892) and Westcott (1901) their Bible continued to change. At first, various American publishers violated British copyright law, printing their own ERV-like Bibles, tailor-making them for American audiences.

In 1928 the "International Council of Religious Education," afraid they'd lose money if the same thing happened to the ASV, bought its copyright from Thomas Nelson.

But it was no use. Though universities and seminaries loved to use the English Revised Version or American Standard Version, the common people still clung to the familiar and preserved words in English, the King James Bible.

But suddenly the winds started to shift.

---

86) A look at my Bible collection revealed that some American printings of the ERV were also made by Thomas Nelson & Sons.

9

THE BIBLE BECOMES ECUMENICAL *UH OH!*

Revised Standard Version (RSV)
New Revised Standard Version (NRS)
English Standard Version (ESV)

CAN'T WE ALL JUST
GET ALONG?

In the early 1900s Protestant theologians got the crazy idea that they could make the earth into God's kingdom, if only the "Christian denominations" could get along with each other.

As an End Times doctrine this is called "Postmillennialism," and it's as old as the Roman Catholic system. As a doctrine of the Church it's called "Ecumenism,"—a horribly deceptive beast of a doctrine.

Ecumenism pretends that you can "leave your beliefs at the door" and get together just as Christians, and everything will be fine. But that is *never* true. Someone's doctrine always wins out. And usually, in one form or another, everyone compromises in favor of the Roman Catholic religion.

Guess what happens when "ecumenically-minded" people decide to come up with a Bible version? Disaster. Chaos. Whatever you call it, one thing you can be sure of: it is nothing like God's preserved words. AMEN!

One of these ecumenical groups was called the "International Council of Religious Education" (ICRE). They knew that the ERV and ASV[87] hardly sold at all, outside of liberal seminaries and universities. But they wanted to make a Bible they could sell to the general public – at least to the people who went to their liberal churches.

So in 1928 they got the copyright for the ASV from Thomas Nelson & Sons. They had decided to make a new translation in 1932, but were stopped cold by the Great Depression.

In 1937 they were able to start again, and they got together 32 big-name "Bible scholars," like James Moffatt and Edgar Goodspeed (each of whom had been making their own Bibles[88]), and well-known Jewish translator Harry Orlinsky.[89]

---

87) For more information on the ERV and ASV, see Chapter 8.
88) Moffatt kept writing and revising editions of *The Bible: A New Translation* between 1922 and 1950. Goodspeed did the same with the Apocrypha and the New Testament for *The Bible: An American Translation* between 1923 and 1948.
89) Jewish translator Orlinsky was dead-set against any Old Testament prophecies that were fulfilled by Jesus Christ. This was obvious from his work on the RSV. He later wrote a book that pretended Jesus could not be prophesied "suffering servant" of Isaiah. Much later he worked on the 1985 NJPS (*New Jewish Publication Society of America Version*) and the 1989 New Revised Standard Version.

THE REVISED STANDARD VERSION
(1946-52)

By 1950 the ICRE and the "Federal Council of Churches" (FCC) had merged into a new group, "the National Council of the Churches of Christ in the USA" (NCC).

Two years later the Revised Standard Version was released on an unsuspecting public. Here are a few surprising points about the RSV:

• Out of the 40 Bible versions investigated for this book, the Revised Standard is the second-worst. The English Revised Version and American Standard Version were bad enough, removing God's words 217 times in my small sample; but the Revised Standard was far worse, removing God's words in 245 out of 257 scripture selections. (See for yourself in Chapter 17.)

• It's one of only three Bibles to completely remove[90] the important words of the angel in Luke 24:6 "He is not here, but is risen…"

• It's one of only five Bibles to remove this crucial historical detail after Jesus' resurrection in Luke 24:40:
    And when he had thus spoken, he shewed
    them his hands and his feet."

• It's one of only four Bibles to completely remove Matthew 12:47:
    Then one said unto him, Behold, thy mother
    and thy brethren stand without, desiring to
    speak with thee.

---

90) By "completely remove" I mean the words aren't even there in italics or in brackets.

DENIES JESUS' POST RESURRECTION, HIS AGONY IN THE GARDEN

• It's one of only *three* Bibles to completely remove Luke 24:12:

> Then arose Peter, and ran unto the sepulchre; and stooping down, he beheld the linen clothes laid by themselves, and departed, wondering in himself at that which was come to pass.

• This is the *only* corroborating testimony to John 20:4-5 regarding Peter going to the tomb after Jesus' resurrection. Don't be fooled. Repetition is important.

• It's one of only *two* Bibles[91] to completely remove Luke 22:43-44:

> And there appeared an angel unto him from heaven, strengthening him. And being in an agony he prayed more earnestly: and his sweat was as it were great drops of blood falling down to the ground.

• We've all heard the term, "the agony in the Garden"? Well, without these verses, there *is* no "agony." This is the *only* place in the Bible that reveals the agony Jesus suffered in the garden of Gethsemane. It is the *only* place in the Bible to tell us about His sweat like blood. It is also the *only* place in the Bible that tells about the angel who strengthened Jesus in the garden, like the angels who ministered unto Him after His three temptations at the beginning of His ministry.[92] MT 4:11 MK 1:13

91) The other one to remove these verses was JB Phillips' *New Testament in Modern English* (1958-72). See Chapter 17.
92) See Matthew 4:11 and Mark 1:13.

• The RSV removes words, phrases and whole verses in 245 of our 257 sample verses. By contrast, the ERV and ASV removed 217. So the RSV removed over 10% more words, phrases and verses than Westcott and Hort could convince the Committee to do with the ERV and ASV. The RSV even removed 8 more words and phrases than the Jehovah's Witnesses did in their New World Translation.

The RSV is not just a "revised King James" at all, is it?

HOW "ECUMENICAL" WAS THE RSV?

Roman Catholic leadership does not permit Catholics to read a book or Bible unless it has the *Nihil Obstat* and/or *Imprimatur* on its copyright page.

• *Nihil Obstat* means "nothing stands in the way" or contradicts the basic Roman Catholic doctrines of popery, idolatry, worship of Mary, earning salvation through works, etc.

• *Imprimatur* means "let it be printed." Catholic leadership declares the book is considered "free from error" in matters of Roman Catholic doctrine and morals, and Catholics are then allowed to read it.

If a publisher can get the *Nihil Obstat* and *Imprimatur*, that can be big money in the bank. You see, compromise seems to pay—at first.

So the National Council of Churches (NCC) went after —and got— that Roman Catholic endorsement.

Here are the results:

- 1957: RSV Apocrypha and Catholic deuterocanoni-cal[93] books published.

- 1965: RSV *New Testament, Catholic Edition*, printed by Thomas Nelson & Sons.

- 1966: RSV *Bible, Catholic Edition*. It arranged the deuterocanonical books in traditional Catholic order, like the so-called "Septuagint."[94]

- 2006: RSV *Bible, 2nd Catholic Edition* (also called the *Ignatius Edition*)

But they didn't just pass off the Catholic RSV on Roman Catholics. At the same time they tried to push Protestants to accept the apocryphal and deuterocanonical books. See for yourself.

- 1965: *RSV Oxford Annotated Bible with the Apocrypha*. It put the Apocrypha at the end of the Bible, after Revelation, between the Bible helps and the map section.

- 1973: *RSV Common Bible, an Ecumenical Edition, with the Apocrypha/Deuterocanonical Books*. It tried to please both Roman Catholics and Greek Orthodox leaders by getting endorsements from their leaders. It also moved the Apocrypha and Deuterocanonical books between the Testaments like the early KJVs did.

---

93) These are uninspired, ancient books that never belonged in the Bible. But when the Protestant Reformation openly rejected them, Catholic leadership quickly raised them to "Deuterocanonical" ("secondary canon") status. Why don't Catholics dump them? Because they use some of the verses in these books to support Catholic doctrines.

94) For more on the so-called "Septuagint," see *Answers to Your Bible Version Questions* (2003), pp. 47-54. Available from Chick Publications.

But unlike the KJV, they *didn't* clearly label each page "Apocrypha" to separate it from the inspired books.

- 1977: *Oxford Annotated Apocrypha, Expanded Edition*. It added 3rd and 4th Maccabees and Psalm 151, used by the Greek Orthodox, to its other apocryphal books.

Can there be any doubt of the RSV's march toward Rome? But the dysfunctional "Revised Standard" family has more than just this…

THE NEW REVISED STANDARD VERSION (1989)

One problem when you start changing the Bible: you don't know where to stop.

Back in 1990, as a seminary graduate and budding linguist I was so excited when I read about the publication of the New Revised Standard Version (NRS). As soon as I read the news article, my wife and I drove down to the nearest Bible bookstore and bought one.

At last. A Bible produced by no less than the famous Greek scholar, Bruce Metzger. Many of my Greek helps in Bible college and seminary had been co-written by him — and so were my Greek New Testaments.

The NRS incorporated all the principles of textual criticism we had been taught, and it read very "smoothly," just like the kind of Bible my wife and I wanted to make as future Bible translators.

But oh, boy. Something was *missing*.

Amazingly, though I tried to put my heart into those words, somehow they came out flat. It was strange. Has someone ever said something to you, and your clear, gut reaction was, "That's wrong," but you could not put your finger on exactly where? That was how I felt.

I'm ashamed to admit it, but my spiritual life dwindled during the time I tried to read that version. I wrote in my journal at the time that this Bible was "spiritually dead" for me. But for the life of me I could not figure out what was wrong.

But now I can tell you what was wrong. They weren't God's words.

It wasn't God's text. And it wasn't God's translation. The Bible didn't say the same thing anymore. It was just the opinions of man written down and passed off as a Bible.

Want a glimpse at what is wrong with the New Revised Standard Version? Let's have a look:

• A lot of "hell" is missing. There are 54 verses in the KJV containing the word "hell." In all but 13 the NRS takes out "hell" and leaves in the untranslated Hebrew word *Sheol* or the Greek word *Hades.* Jesus was unafraid to talk about hell. He talked about hell a lot. What are these guys afraid of?

• Is it any surprise that they also removed words about hell and judgment from Mark 6:11 and 9:45 and completely removed Matthew 21:44, 23:14, Mark 9:44 and 46?[95] There's something about hell that makes these people very nervous.

---

95) Repetition, like you see in Mark 9, is not a "copyist's mistake." It's God's way of emphasizing something important in the Bible. Eliminating repetition is removing God's exclamation point.

• The prophetic nature of Isaiah 7:14 is missing. This verse prophesies of a *virgin* bearing a child, who will be "God with us." God helped Matthew understand this perfectly. Read Matthew 1:23. But the NRS, as the RSV before it, removed "virgin" and put "young woman" to remove the prophecy.

• The "double-brackets" trick: the NRS includes Mark 16:9-20 and John 7:53-8:11, but with a twist —they are in double-brackets [[ ]]. The footnote for John 7:53-8:11 claims "This episode is not found in the most authoritative manuscripts." The footnote[96] for Mark 16:9-20 piles on more doubt, claiming that these verses were "...possibly written in the early second century and appended to the Gospel later in the second century..." They're not trying to explain scripture; they're trying to explain it away.

• From our sample, the NRS is missing 7 less words, phrases and verses than the RSV. Big deal. It still perverts 238, instead of 245 —one more than the Jehovah's Witnesses' New World Translation (NWT).

Even without a *Nihil Obstat* or *Imprimatur*, the *NRSV with Apocrypha* has been welcomed and used by Roman Catholics. Check out required Bible texts at major Catholic universities. You will find the *NRSV with Apocrypha*, alongside the (Roman Catholic) New American, Jerusalem and New Jerusalem Bibles.

It has also been required for courses at mainline Lu-

---

96) This footnote is straight from the *New Oxford Annotated Bible, New Revised Standard Version with the Apocrypha*: *An Ecumenical Study Bible* (3rd edition, 2001).

theran, Anglican, Presbyterian and Methodist universities. The fact that it was the first attempt at a "gender-neutral" Bible helped sway those liberal Protestants, as well.

Yes indeed, the NRS clearly appeals to an ecumenical spirit.

How do you make an ecumenical Bible? You work hard to remove and rewrite anything that makes people feel uncomfortable. That is not easy. A lot of scriptures make people uncomfortable.

It took them years, but the National Council of Churches eventually got their wish. The NRS became the first truly ecumenical Bible.

Why did they work so hard? Because these guys were desperate to make a Bible in their own image, that would "tone down" the gospel and hide the doctrines they hated most, that the King James stated so clearly.

So their Bible pleased almost everybody: their friends, Bible doubters the world over, lukewarm Christians, even the Devil himself...but not God.

THE ENGLISH STANDARD VERSION
(2001)

The English Standard Version (ESV) was a totally different Bible from the RSV and NRS —or so they tell us.

The ESV claims to walk the tightrope between Bible versions. For one thing, it claims to be more literal than the NIV but less literal than the New American Standard.

It removes most, but not all, of the gender-neutral language found in the NRS and Today's NIV (TNIV).

And it puts back most of the words of Old Testament

prophecies that the RSV and NRS perverted to hide their being fulfilled by Jesus Christ in the New Testament.[97]

HOW DIFFERENT IS THE ESV?

Beyond the plastic surgery, is the ESV really that different from the RSV, NRS and other Alexandrian Bibles?

• According to our sample, the ESV is missing only 4 less words, phrases or verses than the NRS. That means they're still 98% the same. Not much of a difference, is it?

• Remember those missing words you read about in Chapters 1, 2, 3 and 6? Check again. They're missing from the ESV, the same as the RSV, NRS and other Alexandrian Bibles.

• All but one of its 234 missing words, phrases and verses from our sample is also missing from either the RSV or NRS. [98]

So while the *translation* of some of the words may be different in the ESV, it is clear that the *text* is just as perverted as the other Alexandrian Bibles.

SEE FOR YOURSELF

Chapter 17 checks 40 Bible versions against the King James Bible, showing 257 verses perverted by missing words or phrases, or just missing entirely.

Check them out for yourself in any version. And keep a

---

97) Of course, this means the ESV still changed some of the prophecies of Christ.
98) The RSV isn't missing the word "Jesus" in 1 Corinthians 5:5. The NRSV isn't missing "on the children of disobedience" from Colossians 3:6. Other than that, every verse of our sample missing words in the ESV is also missing them in the NRS and RSV.

King James Bible handy so you can see the difference. Then ask yourself: which Bible promotes faith in God the Father, in the Lord Jesus Christ His Son, and in the Holy Ghost?

And notice how the other Bibles raise doubts in your heart. You will see for yourself why I trust God's words in the King James Bible.

10

IF IT LOOKS LIKE A DUCK...

- **The New American Standard Version (NAS)**
- **New American Standard 1995 Update (NAU)**

MY STORY

On August 24th, 1980 "I repented of my sins and won the victory." Back then I had two Bibles: a Lamsa Bible,[99] a popular seller in the occultic churches[100] and a gigantic, mule-choking King James Family Tree Bible.

I quickly abandoned the Lamsa and faithfully read my King James daily, starting in both Genesis and Matthew. As big as it was, I knew where my faith lay, and I carried that Book with me everywhere.

---

99) For more about the Lamsa Bible, see *Answers to Your Bible Version Questions* (2003), pp. 163-165. Available from Chick Publications.
100) The Lamsa Bible was popular in "New Thought" churches like Religious Science (where I bought mine) and the so-called Unity School of Christianity (who published many of Lamsa's books).

A well-meaning friend who had talked to me about Christ wanted to relieve me of some of my burden. So, after I was baptized in October of that year, he gave me a gift: a beautiful, brand-new, smaller, easier-to-hold Bible.

I was so excited. Then I looked at the cover: New American Standard.

"What is that?"

> "It's more literal. And it's easier to understand than your other Bible."

Though neither of us knew it at the time, my new Bible started me down the path of doubt that this Bible —or any other on earth— could actually be God's words.

Let me tell you how it happened.

As a newly baptized, repentant believer I longed to understand my new Bible better, so I bought a genuine-leather Ryrie Study Bible, New American Standard. I loved my "Ryrie." I read all the study notes, outlines and indexes faithfully.

A few months later I started going to Bible college. I was on a high. But everything started going downhill after I got my Ryrie. Here's why.

Ryrie's notes often "corrected" the New American Standard, offering a "better" translation. That made it hard to know which to trust: Ryrie or the New American Standard.

At one point I grabbed a Ryrie KJV to see if he liked that translation any better. No way. Ryrie disagreed *even more* with the KJV. So I stuck with my NAS and pressed on.

When I got to Bible college, one of the first things my professors basically said was:

"God's words are perfect. But He entrusted His words to imperfect men. Those words are in writings called the "original autographs." Then men made copies of God's inspired words. But because men aren't perfect, lots of mistakes crept in. But don't worry. The original autographs are perfect and inspired and have no errors. The only thing is, they don't exist anymore. But have no fear: because of the great work of textual scholars of ancient Alexandria and brilliant men from the 1800s to the present, the text that you now have is certified 99 and 44/100% pure. Besides, all Bibles, even the worst copies, are 99% the same."

Oh, there were so many questions in my head I should have asked. But come on, who was I? I was just a "new believer," as they called me.

I was at a disadvantage. I wasn't raised as a Christian like all these other guys. I wasn't trained up like these professors. I figured I was just ignorant or missing something, so I kept my questions to myself. But they didn't go away. Here are some of them:

- If only the "original autographs" are inspired, why didn't God just keep them on earth? People said that we would commit "Bibliolatry" and worship the Bible — but that's a flimsy excuse to me. God had the power to inspire His written words. Couldn't He keep them on earth if they're the only way we can learn the complete truth about God, faith, salvation, heaven and hell?

- If no one has the "original autographs" to check, then how can we know that what we have is "99 and 44/100%" pure? What if all we have are lousy copies?

- If no one has the "original autographs," how can we know we have all the books of the Bible? Or how can we know we don't have one book too many?

- If all the versions of the Bible are "basically the same," why did people hate the King James Bible so much?

Even though one version completely disagreed with another, we were taught to "weigh" the Bibles against each other and "come to our own understanding" of what we thought each verse said. But there was a catch. Wherever it led us was fine, as long as it wasn't to the King James Bible.

I had so many conflicts in my mind that first semester that I came close to flunking out of every class. But in the fall semester, I returned dedicated to be a "good student" and studied my heart out.

I learned that we please our professors by spouting the "party line." And pleasing our professors was how we got good grades. But even though I knew all this, soon I was hooked. I did believe my professors. I became a "true believer" in my favorite teachers, just like other "A" students.

Over the years I moved from the NAS to the ASV, RSV, NEB, NJB and NIV. But I was determined never to trust the KJV. "All Bibles are pretty much as good as one another; *except* the King James."

Never again would I simply take any Bible at its word. Instead, I carried around a backpack full of Greek study helps and Bible versions in English, Greek and Hebrew.

When I did "Bible study" in the New Testament, it got to where I investigated every word, weighing the "authority" of each ancient text, before I would—tentatively—believe I understood a single verse of the Bible.

Brothers and sisters, that's not faith. That is doubt, pure and simple. I have not found a single Bible verse that says we are blessed for doubting God.

Years later, another caring Christian asked some very good questions that sent me on a search for the truth. And within a decade, I was forced to admit from the evidence that God had preserved His words through history,[101] and those preserved words in English are the King James Bible —the same Bible I had started with back in 1980.

Now when I walk around, I don't need a backpack anymore. I just carry God's preserved words in English, the King James Bible —and I know I can believe *every word*.

It took 18 years to undo the work of that one well-meaning Christian. Let this be an example to you, the next time you feel tempted to "make it easier" on a new believer in Christ by giving him or her a corrupted Bible.

THE NASB: ANOTHER BIBLE BUILT UPON A FAULTY FOUNDATION

Some of the greatest evils have started with the best of intentions.

Famous pastor and speaker S. Franklin Logsdon had been friends for years with a well-intentioned businessman: F. Dewey Lockman, founder of the Lockman Foundation.

---

101) God promised to preserve His words through history in Psalm 12:6-7; Matthew 5:18; 24:35; Mark 13:31; Luke 21:33; Deuteronomy 29:29; Isaiah 40:8 and 1 Peter 1:23-25.

PS 12:6-7, MT 5:18, 24:35, MK 13:31, LK 21:33, DEUT 29:29, ISA 40:8, 1PET 1:23-25

Lockman wanted gospel literature and the scriptures distributed to the far corners of the world. With that in mind, he felt he needed to publish the most accurate Bible he could.

MT 7:26-27

That's a wonderful goal. But you should never build a house on a foundation of sand,[102] and Dewey Lockman started with a faulty foundation. Listening to the so-called "scholarship" of the day, he abandoned the King James, God's preserved words for the corrupt words of Westcott and Hort in English —the American Standard Version (ASV 1901).[103]

In 1956-57 his friend Frank Logsdon did a "feasibility study" and interviewed translators to see if it would be a good idea to make a "New" American Standard. Logsdon even wrote the Preface in his enthusiasm. But in the months and years that followed its 1971 publication, Logsdon came to realize he had made a terrible mistake.

Over the next years, Logsdon spoke to churches and wrote to individuals, warning them with these and other words:

> I'm afraid I'm in trouble with the Lord, because I encouraged him [Lockman] to go ahead with it [the New American Standard].

> I must under God renounce every attachment to the New American Standard.

> ...the devil is too wise to try to destroy the Bible.... He can't destroy the word of God. But he can do a lot of things to try to sup-

102) See Matthew 7:26-27.
103) For more on the ASV, see Chapter 8.

plant it, or to corrupt it in the minds and hearts of God's people. Now he can only do it in one of two ways: either by adding to the scriptures or by subtracting from the scriptures....

"The deletions are absolutely frightening."

Lockman and the translators of the NAS began the project with good intentions. Frank Logsdon wrote:

> ...I can aver [declare to be true] that the project was produced by thoroughly sincere men who had the best of intentions. The product, however, is grievous to my heart and helps to complicate matters in these already troublous times. [104]

These men were sincere. But they were sincerely wrong. Why? Because they started with a faulty foundation: the Alexandrian Greek New Testament, the Westcott and Hort English New Testament, and the falsely-called "science" of textual criticism. [105]

WHAT'S MISSING FROM THE NEW AMERICAN STANDARD?

Just from my sample of verses in Chapter 17 (and this is by no means exhaustive) in the New American Standard:

- "*Lord*" is missing 15 times.
- "*Jesus*" is missing 9 times.

---

104) Letter from Franklin Logsdon to Cecil J. Carter, dated June 9, 1977. For more, see two articles by David W. Cloud, "From the NASV to the KJV" and "Did Frank Logsdon Help Organize the New American Standard Version?"
105) See Chapter 7.

- "*Christ*" is missing 30 times.
- "*Jesus Christ*" or "*Christ Jesus*" is missing 4 times
- "*Lord Jesus Christ*" is missing 3 times

People not raised on the KJV are growing to doubt that Jesus Christ is God, that Christ is Lord and even the clear Bible doctrine that He is the only way to heaven.[106] You cannot deny it: the Devil's plan is working.

Remember this: Satan doesn't want *every* word omitted; it would be too obvious. Instead, he wants to fuel your doubts about the doctrines of the verses that are left. As Frank Logsdon put it, "It is done so subtly that very few would discover it."

Does it work? The proof is all around you. Look at the church today. What doctrines are more Evangelicals and others having the greatest problems believing? They are the very doctrines that Satan meant to chip away at, by taking out words, phrases and verses in ancient Alexandrian and modern Bibles.

Here are some more examples from our sampling of verses:

- In Luke 4:8, Jesus' command to the devil, "Get thee behind me, Satan," is missing.
- In Mark 9:29; Acts 10:30 and 1 Corinthians 7:5 "fasting" is missing.
- In Matthew 17:21, "prayer and fasting" are both missing.[107]

---

106) See Matthew 7:21-23; John 3:16-18; 14:6; Acts 4:12, 1 Timothy 6:14-15.
107) In the NAS, this verse is put in brackets. But see the next section, "Brackets in the New American Standard."

[handwritten marginal note, right margin: MT 7:21-23; JN 3:16-18; 14:6; ACTS 4:12; 1 TIM 6:14-15]

[handwritten marginal note, left margin: DO WE DON'T NEED TO FAST/PRAY? GET BEHIND ME SATAN? NO]

Margin handwritten note (rotated, left side): NO HELL? No ASCENSION OF JESUS?

- "Hell" has almost disappeared, reduced from 54 verses to only 15. Words from Mark 9:45 and all of 9:44 and 46, where Christ repeated Himself in exclaiming the dangers of hell, have been removed as well.

Is it any wonder that doctrines about Satan, prayer, fasting, and the existence and nature of hell, are questioned and doubted by modern preachers, teachers and youth?

- In Luke 24:51, the statement about Jesus' ascension, "and [was] carried up into heaven," is missing. But Luke himself, by the inspiration of God, told us he wrote these words. In Acts 1:1-2 Luke wrote: "The former treatise have I made" (referring to the Gospel of Luke) "of all that Jesus began both to do and to teach ...until the day in which he was taken up...." How could God make it more obvious that these words belong? But the NAS translators trusted Westcott and Hort and their "textual criticism," relying on one of their favorite texts, Codex Sinaiticus—even though almost every other manuscript in the world has those words. Should we trust these "scholars," or what God has preserved?

BRACKETS IN THE
NEW AMERICAN STANDARD

As you saw in Chapter 4, there are no brackets in the King James Bible. Every word was placed in it with care because the translators believed those were the very words of God, translated accurately into English.

But in the New American Standard, brackets have a sneaky aim. This is how the NAS describes its use of brackets:

[ ] Brackets in the text are around words probably *not* in the original writings.[108]

In other words, the NAS translators put brackets when they did not believe the words they put in their Bible. What does that do to your faith in those words? How would you ever believe what they say is true? Inside the first bracket, they put a "1" to make you look at their margin: ([1]) Then the margin says this: [1] Many mss. do not contain this v. [This is short for "Many manuscripts do not contain this verse.]

It looks like they want you to disbelieve those words, even though they are God's words, contained in preserved Bibles throughout history.

• Out of the 47 verses in which brackets are found in my small sample, 41 of the 47 are whole verses. So they didn't believe those 41 verses, yet they put them in their Bible so you would buy their book. How dishonest can you get?

In Bible college I was told over and over again, "The New American Standard is the conservative Christian response to the Revised Standard Version."

But is the NAS more conservative? Out of our sample, it perverts 7 less verses than the RSV, but that's still 238 out of 257 perverted verses —identical to the number perverted in the New Revised Standard. That's hardly what I would call "conservative." But they took another try at it in 1995. Did it get any better?

---

108) This is from *The Ryrie Study Bible, New American Standard Translation* (1976, 78), p. xi. Emphasis mine. Words vary slightly between NAS Bibles.

THE NEW AMERICAN STANDARD 1995 UPDATE

Why was an "update" done to the New American Standard? What changed? Well, in this book we want to focus on what is missing. [109] So let's compare.

The NAU's missing words, phrases and verses affect 6 less verses than the NAS. But that is still 232 out of the 257 selected verses. Here are the verses the NAU tried to "fix" to remove obvious NAS errors: [110]

- In Luke 24:36, it put back Jesus' words "and saith unto them, Peace be unto you."

- In Mark 14:68, it put back the historical fact, "and the cock crew."

- It put back the whole verse of Luke 24:12 about Peter visiting the sepulchre. In the NAS it was in brackets.

- It put back the whole verse of Luke 24:40 about Jesus showing His hands and feet. In the NAS they were in brackets and had the note, "Many mss. do not contain this v." But in the NAU the note was completely removed. So what happened to those "many mss." they thought were so important before?

- It fixed their embarrassing removal of the ascension of Jesus "and [was] carried up into heaven" in Luke 24:51, and again they took away the negative note.

---

109) There is so much to tell you about what's *changed* in the NAS, but I'll have to do that in another book.

110) Funny, but 4 of those 6 "fixed" verses in the NAU all come out of Luke 24. Why did they take so much out of that important chapter to begin with? Something must have happened to change their minds and get them to agree with the King James. But their notes are totally silent.

- In Colossians 3:6, it put back that the wrath of God cometh "on the children of disobedience," and changed the note from "some early mss. have" it, to the more honest "two early mss. do not contain" the words.

So only 6 of our sample verses are actually different in the NAU. But 232 of them are just as bad as the NAS. How different is it, really? *NOT MUCH!*

Every one of those changes was something the King James Bible already said. So which are you going to trust, a Bible that needs change, or one that has never changed?

I don't want to be fooled by so-called "scholarship" twice. I'm sticking with God's preserved words in English, the King James Bible.

The next time someone says the New American Standard is a "conservative" or "perfectly acceptable" translation," remember how it removes more of God's words than almost all the other translations (in our list it's #4), almost as bad as the "liberal" RSV and just as bad as the NRS.

Remember that old saying: "If it looks like a duck, walks like a duck and quacks like a duck ... it's a duck."

11

The "International" Bibles:

- **New International Version (NIV)**
- **Today's NIV (TNIV)**
- **New International Reader's Version (NIrV)**

SOMETHING FOR NOTHING?

I attended Bible college from 1981-1984. During that time there was a kind of "hand out" that happened at the beginning of every school year. Somewhere near the classrooms would be a guy handing out brand-new, full-size, large-margin (for notes), hard-cover NIV Bibles. For free.

Who could resist an offer like that? The only thing missing were the maps in the back, but we didn't care. Make something free and college students will climb through sewer grates to grab it.

Of course, you know how it goes. "The first one's free, but the next one's gonna cost you." Once professors started using the NIV (probably starting with free copies like us), we had to have other study helps using the NIV as well.

For years the KJV was the only game in town. To search the entire Bible you needed either a Strong's or Young's Concordance to find every word. But the NAS was starting to make its own concordance, and the NIV people were quickly on the move.

Before I saw what was happening, I was shelling out big bucks for costly books like:

- The NIV Greek-English Interlinear New Testament
- The NIV Hebrew-English Interlinear Old Testament (all four volumes.) DANG!
- The NIV Study Bible
- Other study helps, because they used the NIV as well.

I actually bought an NIV Greek-English Interlinear New Testament for my wife for the anniversary of our engagement. The bookstore clerk said, "That's not very romantic." I responded, "To Deb it is." (Okay, so it wasn't a typical romance. But you get the idea.)

Later on, with the money I got for tutoring Greek, I bought 25 NIV Bibles to give away. With other money, I bought NIV Study Bibles and the Lutherans' Concordia NIV Self-Study Bibles to give to friends.

Alright, I was a sucker. But a well-intentioned one.

Those "free Bibles" must have cost them mega-bucks. The NIV publishers sure invested in us Bible college students. But we should have realized that you never get something for nothing. Everything costs.

As time went on, we heard about other colleges that got the same "free Bibles." But in the end, that huge investment by the publishers sure paid off. The NIV became one of the most-purchased Bibles in the world.

SOMETHING FOR EVERYONE?

It's called the New "International" Version for a reason. According to the Preface in my free NIV[111] it started in 1965 after some committees from the Christian Reformed Church and the National Association of Evangelicals decided a totally new translation was necessary:

> That they were from many denominations—including Anglican, Assemblies of God, Baptist, Brethren, Christian Reformed, Church of Christ, Evangelical Free, Lutheran, Mennonite, Methodist, Nazarene, Presbyterian, Wesleyan and other churches—helped to safeguard the translation from sectarian bias.

Our denomination was in the list. It must be good, right? But that's not all:

> The fact that participants from the United States, Great Britain, Canada, Australia and New Zealand worked together gave the project its international scope.

Yes, Brothers and Sisters. It was "scholarly," too.

> In 1967 the New York Bible Society (now the New York International Bible Society) generously undertook the financial sponsorship of

---

111) This information comes from the Preface to the wide-margin NIV, 3rd printing, December 1978, pp. vii-xi.

the project—a sponsorship that made it possible to enlist the help of many distinguished scholars.

I want you to note something very important:

All this involved many thousands of hours of research and discussion regarding the meaning of the texts and the precise way of putting them into English. It may well be that no other translation has been made by a more thorough process of review and revision from committee to committee than this one.

When I show you words that are missing from the NIV that are clearly in God's preserved Bibles throughout history —a couple of which are in every single manuscript I can find, including the Alexandrian ones— I want you to remember that every word in the NIV was put there intentionally, with a great deal of thought.

There you have it. It is trans-denominational, international, and "scholarly." It's got something for everyone. What more could anyone want in a Bible version?

What I want is what God actually said. So let's see how the NIV measured up.

SOMETHING IS MISSING

To say "Something is missing" from the NIV is an understatement. Of the 40 Bibles investigated for this book and based on my sample of 257 verses, the NIV is missing more words, phrases and whole verses than *any other* Bible version. The NIV tops the list with 246 out of 257 verses perverted by deleting God's holy and preserved words.

It's always important when you remove a word that God intended to be in the Bible. But there is no reason to remove the simple and obvious name "Jesus" from these verses. See for yourself:

> (Matthew 17:22) And while they abode in Galilee, ~~Jesus~~ said unto them, The Son of man shall be betrayed into the hands of men:

> (Mark 14:18) And as they sat and did eat, ~~Jesus~~ said, Verily I say unto you, One of you which eateth with me shall betray me.

First, these verses are so obviously about Jesus that a three-year-old with a good attention span could see that.

Second, every Greek manuscript in the known universe contains the Lord's name "Jesus." So why did they take it out? The NIV bragged about its "scholars" and attention to detail. Did one of them think the style was better by removing what God had placed there? None of 38 other Bible versions removed the Lord's name there. What gave them the gall to do this? DANG!

This may seem like such a tiny thing. It took me a lot of hours of intense study to even find it. But there it is. And it shows you an attitude. If they are willing, without remorse, to take out something that exists in every single Greek text, what more of God's words are they willing to remove? The clear answer is: a lot.

- It also removes "the Lord" from Luke 17:6, present in *every* Greek manuscript.

- In 1 Corinthians 9:18, the NIV and three other versions not only remove that it is the gospel "of Christ," but also delete the 2nd and 3rd times Paul repeated "gospel" in that verse, though it is present in *every* Greek manuscript.

- 16 whole verses are completely missing. DANG!

THE ONLY ... WHAT?

The fact that Jesus is God's only "begotten" Son is removed from the NIV New Testament. Yet they use the term in Isaiah 45:10 without apology. This term is important. We are "adopted" sons, but we are not "begotten." Only Jesus was "begotten" of God the Father. That is one way we describe how He is God and we are not.

So it is no minor thing that the NIV led the pack in dropping this important word and taking away this vital doctrine of God the Son along with it.

What is their problem with Jesus? The NIV can't seem to decide who He is. In 1978 John 1:18 said Jesus was "God the only [Son]." By 1984 He became "God the one and only." But both are wrong. Jesus is "the only begotten Son," just like it says in the King James Bible and the vast majority of ancient Greek manuscripts.

The NIV eliminates a number of other vital things about our Lord Jesus Christ:

- It eliminates that He was Mary's "firstborn" son in Matthew 1:25.

- It eliminates that He is "the beginning and the ending" in Revelation 1:8.

- It eliminates that He is "the Alpha and the Omega, the first and the last" in Revelation 1:11.

- It eliminates "and art to come," part of the future nature of Christ in Revelation 11:17.
- It eliminates that our belief must be "on me," on Jesus, to have everlasting life in John 6:47.
- It completely removes Acts 8:37, the only verse in the Bible that says what one must do before he can be baptized —believe with all your heart that Jesus Christ is the Son of God. (See Chapter 2.)
- It completely removes from Matthew 9:13 and Mark 2:17 what Jesus Christ came to call sinners to do: He came to call them "to repentance."
- It completely removes Mark 15:28, the only place in the Bible that states how Jesus fulfilled Isaiah 53:12.
- All sorts of historical details concerning the life of Christ and the early Church are omitted from the NIV, as well. Are we really going to trust these committees against the entire history of God's preserved words? Do we want to take that chance with God?

Chapter 17 is filled with verses that have been perverted or removed entirely by the NIV and 39 other Bibles. As you will see for yourself, the NIV appears on the list more than any other Bible version.

Take a close look at what this Bible, and the others listed, are missing. Do you think that with all those words, phrases and verses missing, none of them is important, none of them is about an important doctrine? That's what professors and even some preachers have been telling us.

But as for me, I'll trust what God revealed and preserved for thousands of years over any scholar, any day. As He Himself revealed through the Psalmist:

> It is better to trust in the LORD than to put confidence in man. It is better to trust in the LORD than to put confidence in princes[112]

PS 118.89

TODAY'S NIV: A SNEAKY WAY TO KEEP A PROMISE

In 1997, it was revealed that the International Bible Society (IBS) in Britain had quietly copyrighted an "Inclusive Language Edition" of the NIV back in 1995. This version removed and changed gender words such as man, father, son, he, she, etc. Take a look at 1 Corinthians 15:21 for example.

ADAM

> KJV For since by man came death, by man came also the resurrection of the dead. *CHRIST*

The first "man" is Adam. The second "man" is Christ Jesus.

WHO?

> NIVI (&TNIV) For since death came through a human being, the resurrection of the dead comes also through a human being. *WHO?*

What possible reason could there be for removing the fact that Adam and Christ were both men? This was done simply to make the Bible more "inclusive" of the feminine gender, even in places where the Greek and Hebrew clearly are masculine. *FEMINISTS LOVE THAT!*

Quickly, the Southern Baptist Convention, James Dobson and others who used the NIV openly criticized

---

112) Psalm 118:8-9.

this proposed change. On May 27, the IBS claimed they would stop all consideration of gender-related changes to the NIV, stating in a press conference:

> IBS has abandoned all plans for gender-re-lated changes in future editions of the New International Version (NIV).

> The present (1984) NIV text will continue to be published. There are no plans for a further revised edition.

> IBS will begin immediately to revise the New International Readers Version (NIrV) in a way that reflects the treatment of gender in the NIV. IBS is directing the licensees who publish the current NIrV to publish only the revised NIrV edition as soon as it is ready.

> IBS will enter into negotiations with the publisher of the NIV in the U.K. on the matter of ceasing publication of its "inclusive language" edition of the NIV.

History shows they kept their promise —well, sort of.

By May of 1999, the IBS and its Committee on Bible Translation (CBT) announced it would keep working and possibly produce a new English translation, but not called the NIV.

In June a previously un-released letter from 1999 re-vealed that they fully supported "gender-accurate lan-guage," stating, "The matter is one of timing, of finding the appropriate hour to move ahead."[113] In a few days another

---

113) "There They Go Again" by Susan Olasky, *World* magazine, June 5, 1999.

article appeared,[114] reporting this Bible was due to be published in 2003 or 2004. It pointed out:

- It will not be called the NIV, but will have a similar name.

- "The style and character will remain the same" as the NIV.

- The Committee on Bible Translation (CBT) that originally translated the NIV would do the research on the wording of this new version.

So, in fits and starts, with accusations and denials, somewhere between January of 2002 and 2005, "Today's NIV" (as you can see, a "major" name change) was published.

WHAT'S MISSING FROM THE TNIV?

Pretty much everything missing in the NIV is also missing in the TNIV. Check Chapter 17 and see for yourself.

- It is also missing Jesus' name in those two verses, Matthew 17:22 and Mark 14:18, that every single text in the world but the NIV has. It's not really surprising, is it?

- It has perverted 242 of the 257 verses listed in this book, 4 verses less than the NIV. Big, whopping difference.

- This number makes the TNIV the third-worst Bible of the 40 reviewed for this book.

---

114) "'Gender-accurate' Bible soon to be published," *Religion Today*, June 24, 1999.

- This is our Hall of Shame so far, in terms of verses perverted from our sample:

  - NIV   246   New International Version
  - RSV   245   Revised Standard Version
  - TNIV 242   Today's NIV
  - NAS   238   New American Standard
  - NRS   238   New Revised Standard
  - NWT   237   Jehovah's Witness New World
               Translation

As you can see from the numbers, the New World Translation of the Jehovah's Witnesses is in fifth place, behind these Protestant Bibles. Do you want a Bible that is worse than the one the Jehovah's Witnesses use? I don't.

THE NEW INTERNATIONAL READER'S VERSION (NIrV)

As you have seen already, in 1996 an early edition of the NIrV had been made "inclusive-language," but in mid-1997 the International Bible Society promised to rewrite it to conform to what they called "NIV standards."

In 1998 the revision was published, and people pretty much quieted down about this simplified Bible geared to children and people for whom English was a second or other language.

WHAT'S MISSING FROM THE NIrV?

Because the NIrV is basically a simplified English Bible, it had to state things in simple sentences. So by accident, a lot of words that the NIV took out had to be put right back in the text where they belong. But even so, out of 40 Bibles, the NIrV still took 7th place, perverting 232 of our sample of 257 verses, just as many as the New American Standard 1995 Update (NAU). [115]

The "New International Version" family of Bibles has endured its share of controversy. But that isn't what is important. We have to look behind the scenes at what is really happening. Satan got his way: people have already accepted the perverted Greek Bibles of Alexandria and the Greek and English texts of Westcott and Hort and rejected the words of God that God Himself promised to preserve.

It's amazing. More words, phrases and verses are removed from the NIV than any other Bible, and yet people want their Bibles to be "as conservative as the NIV."

What an amazing con job.

NIV IS ALSO BEST SELLING OF THE NEW VERSIONS

115) See Chapter 10 for more on the NAU.

12

Error Paraphrased:

- The Living Bible (LB)
- New Living Translation (NLT)

MORE GOOD INTENTIONS... WITH THE SAME FAULTY FOUNDATION

Just like Lockman, Logsdon and the New American Standard, the Living Bible was started out by a man with the greatest of intentions.

Dr. Kenneth Taylor wanted a Bible that was easier to read than the King James Bible. So he set out to make a paraphrase for his kids. And what Bible did he make his foundation? The same one the New American Standard used: the American Standard 1901 (ASV).

Somewhere between his Master's degree and his honorary doctorates, Ken Taylor said he was taught that the ASV was "the most accurate of the word-for-word English translations" and was "prepared by a large committee of scholars far more expert in Greek than I was." So abandoning God's preserved words, he trusted some scholars who perverted or removed the historical text of the Bible in thousands of places. * EDUCATED FOOL!*

Let's face it. An easy-to-read lie is still a lie.

He started with *Living Letters* in 1962, then eventually paraphrased the entire New Testament in 1967 and the Old Testament in 1971. So now people had Ken Taylor's paraphrase of Westcott and Hort's perverted Bible.

After Billy Graham pushed the book into fame and fortune for Kenneth Taylor and his Tyndale House Publishing, Taylor decided to make a Roman Catholic edition, as well, to help along people trying to understand the Jesuit Douay-Rheims Bible.

After a Roman Catholic priest translated the Apocrypha to his liking, Taylor had *The Catholic Living Bible* published and got both the *Imprimatur* and *Nihil Obstat*. [116] With those Catholic endorsements, the Catholic Living Bible also became a success.

When I was studying Spanish in Cuernavaca, Morelos, Mexico in 1981, I saw plenty Spanish Catholic Living Bibles and Catholic Today's English Version (Good News) Bibles for sale in local stores. I was amazed how all of a sudden I was seeing so many Protestant Bibles re-made with an Apocrypha for the Catholic people. *CHRISTIAN UNITY?*

Why not? There was big money to be made. Besides, there wasn't any real difference between the Protestant and

---

116) See Chapter 9.

Catholic Bible texts from 1979 onward. Both used Westcott and Hort's perverted Alexandrian-type text. So what's the difference?

WHAT'S MISSING FROM THE LIVING BIBLE?

The Living Bible is by nature a paraphrase, so lots of things "Bible critics" took out ended up right back in the text, just out of the need to make things clear. But out of our 257 chosen verses, the Living Bible clearly perverts 156 of them.

In addition, there are still plenty of footnotes, each telling why this or that word or phrase does not belong in the text, but the text itself had the words. Still, 156 is an awful lot of verses with God's holy words removed, even if it is 61 less than the ERV and ASV.

But the "scholars" changed all that with the New Living Translation. DID THEY?

THE NEW LIVING TRANSLATION

In 1989, 90 Evangelical "scholars" met to correct the Living Bible. But soon that aim was abandoned, and instead they worked to create a "new" Living Translation.

They decided to use the Greek and Hebrew the Catholics and Protestants agreed upon, the United Bible Society's 4th Revised Greek New Testament (1993) and the *Biblia Hebraica Stuttgartensia* (1977), both published at the Vatican and in Germany.

Why not? As I said, they already agreed on the texts. All that was left was the translation (and a few apocryphal books, of course).

By 2004 the New Living Translation was released, at first almost silly in its "gender neutrality." They had to keep revising the text, it seems, to keep ahead of the criticisms. Here are three versions of part of Acts 1:21, from oldest to newest:

- "So now we must choose someone else to take Judas' place…" (2004)

- "So now we must choose another man to take Judas's place…" (about 2006)

- "So now we must choose a replacement for Judas from among the men..." (2nd Edition, current in 2009)

The present edition is a lot less gender-neutral, but does it contain more of God's words?

WHAT'S MISSING FROM THE NEW LIVING TRANSLATION?

What started out to be a "corrected" Living Bible quickly deleted enough words, phrases and verses to make it tie for 11th place in our list of Bible perversions. In short, it deletes words in 225 of our selection of 257 verses, 8 more than Westcott and Hort got into the ERV and ASV.

When it comes down to it, I don't want lies, whether accurately quoted or paraphrased. I just want to have in my hands the words that God said, that God Himself promised to preserve. So I'll keep my King James Bible and pray to God for understanding, rather than trust these wise-guy "scholars" to delete and reinterpret God's words for me according to their own whims.

And you can paraphrase that any way you want.

13

THE "PICK AND CHOOSE" BIBLE:

• **The Amplified Bible (AMP)**

THE VERSE THAT WOULD
NOT END

Have you ever heard the Amplified Bible read from the pulpit? The preacher has brought his Bibles and notes, and is very excited to tell you what he has learned. You open your King James Bible and read the text:

Romans 10:4 For Christ is the end of the law for righteousness to every one that believeth.

But the person behind the pulpit states in a scholarly tone, "To help you appreciate the depth of the nuances of these words, I want you to hear them again, in the Amplified Bible." And this is what you hear:

"For Christ is the end of the Law [the limit at which it ceases to be, for the Law leads up to Him Who is the fulfillment of its types, and in Him the purpose which it was designed to

108

accomplish is fulfilled. That is, the purpose of the Law is fulfilled in Him] as the means of righteousness (right relationship to God) for everyone who trusts in and adheres to and relies on Him."

Huh? This is supposed to be clearer than the simple words of the King James? Who are they kidding? They just blew up a 15-word verse to a whopping 75 words. And after all that, do you have a clue what it means? (Try reading it out loud and see if that helps.)

But there is another result of reading the Amplified Bible that we don't notice so quickly.

THE READER THAT BECOMES THE BIBLE TRANSLATOR

Suppose I were to come up to you and say:

"I was mad about the flat."

If you were a 21st century American, you would interpret those words to mean I was "mad" (very upset) that my tire was no longer round. I would have to spend the next frustrating minutes of my life (or longer) getting tools out of my vehicle, jacking up my auto and removing the deflated tire, only to spend more wasted minutes (or longer) searching through the hot, scorching sun for a service station.

However, if you were a 21st century British person, you would interpret those words to mean I was "mad" (thrilled) about the "flat" (apartment) I had just rented.

Both of those meanings are equally valid, given the right circumstances. If I were in the scorching Arizona desert or in front of the Queen's palace, you would know exactly which one was meant.

The same is true in Bible study. Just because a word can mean different things in various circumstances does not mean that it must mean all of them, or any of them, in a certain Bible verse. We must look to the words and verses surrounding it (the context) to find out which meaning is correct. Bible believers through history have done this when they translated God's preserved words.

But look at how the Amplified Bible refers to the Lord Jesus in John 1:18. I put in bold type the words we are focusing on:

> No man has ever seen God at any time; **the only unique Son** or **the only begotten God,** Who is in the bosom [in the intimate presence] of the Father, He has declared Him [He has revealed Him and brought Him out where He can be seen; He has interpreted Him and He has made Him known].

(handwritten margin note: TRANSLATORS DON'T BELIEVE Jesus IS THE Son of GOD!)

There are so many things wrong with this verse. Here are a few:

- "Son" is correct, but they put it in italics, meaning they don't believe it. *(handwritten: YUP!)*
- "Begotten" is correct, but they put it with the wrong word, "God."
- They have only supplied two possible readings, and both of them are wrong. The correct, historical and preserved words are "the only begotten Son," —but it's nowhere in the text, not in so much as a footnote.

(handwritten margin note: BEGOTTEN GOD? OR BEGOTTEN SON?)

This translation forces you to become a Bible translator, a Greek and Hebrew scholar and theologian all rolled up in one, and choose for yourself which reading they provided that you think is correct.

Is that what a Bible is supposed to do? No way!

THOSE IRRITATING ITALICS

When I have read an Amplified Bible out loud, I've never known quite what to do to make the italics obvious with my voice. Do I yell them, whisper them, or do I turn my head sort of sideways, or slant my hands, so people know I am reading italicized words? It's pretty clear that the Amplified Bible was made to be a reader's Bible, not a speaker's Bible.

But oh, those italics hide a dark secret.

Let's look at the Introduction to a 1987 copy of The Amplified Bible, page viii:

> Italics point out:
>
> …Certain familiar passages now recognized as not adequately supported by the original manuscripts. That is the primary use of italics in the New Testament, so that, upon encountering italics, the reader is alerted to a matter of textual readings….

It doesn't matter how "familiar" the words are. If they don't belong in the Bible, we shouldn't put them there. Why would anyone do that?

The answer is simple: "marketability." Who will buy a Bible missing their favorite verses? Not many. They're not dumb. They want you to buy their Bible. So, to maintain their "scholarly integrity" and still make a profit, they put your favorite words (that they do not believe) in italics.

But what about the passages that aren't so "familiar"? Ah ha! That's where they can delete words to their heart's content —and hope you don't notice.

Believe it or not, with the Amplified Bible, most people don't notice a thing. They still think the Amplified Bible is some kind of ramped-up King James. But wait till they find out what's missing.

WHAT'S MISSING FROM THE AMPLIFIED BIBLE?

When I first went through the Amplified Bible, I used an online version instead of one of my hardback Bibles. As I checked all 257 verses, I found 82 missing words, phrases or whole verses. That's still important, because every single word of God is important, but it's 37th out of the 40 Bibles.

But for some reason I had to look something up in a hardback Amplified Bible, and suddenly the numbers rose dramatically. How? It turns out that the online version doesn't show any italics! NO ITALICS?!

So how many verses are perverted by the words, phrases or whole verses being in italics? 112, and with 7 other ways they state that the words and verses do not belong, the total comes up to 201 out of 257 verses perverted in the Amplified Bible, only 16 less than Westcott and Hort's Bibles.

That's 201 verses totally out-of-line with the preserved words of God, 78% of our sample verses.

Brothers and Sisters, that's no King James *anything*.

DO WE NEED A "MULTIPLE-CHOICE" BIBLE?

As I read the Bible, there are many things I don't want to know:

- I don't want to read multiple choices of what God could have said.
- I don't want to read what men say God might mean.
- I don't want to read what men think God should have said.

I just want to know what God said. And I trust His Holy Spirit to guide me into all truth. That is as "amplified" a Bible as I need.

14

A COUNTERFEIT MESSAGE

• The Message Bible (MSG)

THE PROBLEM WITH PARAPHRASES

You are sitting in Bible study and the leader asks you to read John 3:5. You open your King James Bible and read:

> Jesus answered, Verily, verily, I say unto thee, Except a man be born of water and *of* the Spirit, he cannot enter into the kingdom of God.

But the leader is not satisfied. He asks, "Does anyone else have another translation?" One person raises her hand and says, "I have *The Message Bible*." The leader is intrigued. All sorts of famous people from all walks of life have been endorsing that version. "Go ahead and read that to us," the leader says. So she reads:

GOD WAS A CREATION?!

Jesus said, "You're not listening. Let me say it again. Unless a person submits to this original creation—the 'wind hovering over the water' creation, the invisible moving the visible, a baptism into a new life--it's not possible to enter God's kingdom."

An awkward silence.

Eventually the conversation starts again, and people continue to read, through John 3:16. The study leader thinks, "This is one of the most important verses in the Bible. I've got to hear how this verse is translated in the *Message*."

So the woman is asked to read again. You quickly recite in your mind the most familiar verse in the whole Bible:

> For God so loved the world, that he gave his only begotten Son, that whosoever believeth in him should not perish, but have everlasting life.

Then the woman opens her Message Bible and reads:

> This is how much God loved the world: He gave his Son, his one and only Son. And this is why: so that no one need be destroyed; by believing in him, anyone can have a whole and lasting life.

WHAT ABOUT ETERNAL LIFE

The leader can take it no more. "Are you sure that's what it says? May I see that?" He reads the *Message* for himself. That's exactly what it says. Quickly he teaches a lesson so everyone can understand what is wrong:

1. Jesus is God's "only begotten" Son. He is not

Handwritten top margin: JN 1:12; ROM 8:14; GAL 3:26; 4:6, 1 JN 3:1-2

God's "one and only" Son, because we are all God's adopted sons by faith in Jesus.[117]

2. The unsaved will not be destroyed. They will exist forever in the lake of fire.[118]

Handwritten: MT 25:46; 2 PT 2:9,17; JUDE 11-13 REV 20:10, 14-15

3. God is not promising a "whole and lasting life" *21:8* in the present. He is promising "everlasting life" into eternity. (Romans 5:21; 6:23). And 1 Corinthians 15:19 says:

> If in this life only we have hope in Christ, we are of all men most miserable."

"That is the problem with paraphrases," the leader concludes. "You find out what the author wants to say, but not what God actually said."

GETTING CREATIVE WITH THE TRUTH

We love to hear someone retell a story that he or she heard. It's fun to hear different people tell the same story, as well. Each person has some different nuance to share. Some are subtle, some hold you in suspense, and others make you laugh.

But unless the story is very basic, most will leave out a detail here or there. That's normal. We expect that. But we can't have important details left out when we are dealing with God's words. God had a reason for every single word He put in His Bible. Want an example?

Let me talk about a serious issue. There is a whole

---

117) John 1:12; Romans 8:14; Galatians 3:26; 4:6; 1 John 3:1-2.
118) Matthew 25:46; 2 Peter 2:9, 17; Jude 1:11-13; Revelation 20:10, 14-15; 21:8.

movement of people that wants to steal the hearts—and take away the purity—of your children. The lesbian/gay/bisexual/transgender/questioning (LGBTQ) movement is like an army that wants your kids in the worst way.[119]

What do you do when your kids ask you to open *The Message Bible* and answer that important question, "What does God say about homosexuality?" See for yourself:

King James Bible, Romans 1:27

> And likewise also the men, leaving the natural use of the woman, burned in their lust one toward another; men with men working that which is unseemly, and receiving in themselves that recompence of their error which was meet.

The Message, Romans 1:27

> Sexually confused, they abused and defiled one another, women with women, men with men--all lust, no love. And then they paid for it, oh, how they paid for it--emptied of God and love, godless and loveless wretches.

The words, "the men, leaving the natural use of the woman, burned in their lust one toward another" are absolutely clear. But *The Message Bible* simply talks about "women with women, men with men" "abus[ing] and defil[ing] one another." Then it adds, "all lust, no love." Any gay or lesbian couple who read that would say they are not "abusing" or "defiling" each other, because they love each other.

---

119) For more information, see *Hot Topics* (2008), pp. 6-31. Available from Chick Publications.

A CAY BIBLE?!

The Message may be poetic or "tolerant," but it's not what God said. It won't help answer your child's question.

What about 1 Corinthians 6:9-10 in *The Message Bible*? Guess what? Homosexuality is completely missing from those verses.

And what about the carefully detailed list of sins God gave Paul in 1 Timothy 1:9-10? Take a look:

King James Bible   1 Timothy 1:9-10

> 9 Knowing this, that the law is not made for a righteous man, but for the lawless and disobedient, for the ungodly and for sinners, for unholy and profane, for murderers of fathers and murderers of mothers, for manslayers
>
> 10 For whoremongers, for them that defile themselves with mankind, for menstealers, for liars, for perjured persons, and if there be any other thing that is contrary to sound doctrine;

The Message 1 Timothy 1:9-10

> 9 It's obvious, isn't it, that the law code isn't primarily for people who live responsibly, but for the irresponsible, who defy all authority, riding roughshod over God, life,
>
> 10 sex, truth, whatever!

Wow! Can you believe it? A list of specific sins in the real Bible becomes "whatever" in *The Message Bible*. The most it says is "riding roughshod over …sex."

A gay or lesbian, bisexual or transgender person could say, "See? I don't 'ride roughshod over sex' —I have a caring, committed relationship, so it's not about me." And we would have nothing to say.

Again, if we search in *The Message* for God's thoughts about homosexuality we come up empty. Brothers and Sisters, when we teach Bible doctrine is not the time to get "creative" with the truth.

Please understand what I am saying. There is nothing wrong with being creative, even with creative storytelling. It's wonderful —in its place. But the Bible is the truth. Let's not change the truth of God into a lie (Romans 1:25). It is no accident that the phrase, "getting creative with the truth" is a nice way of saying someone is "telling a lie."

IS "THE MESSAGE" A BIBLE?

Some people say, "Why are you being so hard on *The Message*? It's not even a Bible." Others say, "The *Message* is a paraphrase, not a translation." Still others go further, saying it's only a kind of preaching help, a "homiletical tool." There are so many opinions. It's obvious that people are confused about how to classify *The Message*. Let's see if NavPress, the publisher, can clear this up.

On the back cover of my hardback copy, it says:

> …The Message, Eugene Peterson's best-selling paraphrasing translation of the Bible…

That's *really* confusing. Is it a paraphrase, or a translation? It can't be both, can it? Let's look at the front cover:

> The Bible in Contemporary Language, The Message, Eugene H. Peterson

It says "the Bible." Can anyone deny it? But it also gives the name of Eugene Peterson as the author. Can man take credit as the author of God's words? Not according to my Bible. Let's open *The Message* and look inside:

> The Message is a contemporary rendering of the Bible from the original languages, crafted to present its tone, rhythm, events, and ideas in everyday language.

"From the original languages" is what we say when we're making a translation. The copyright page says...

> Thank you for purchasing a copy of THE MESSAGE Bible...

It's clearly called a Bible. And when you want to quote from "*THE MESSAGE* text," it says you "must" use these words "as follows":

> "Scripture taken from THE MESSAGE. Copyright ©1993, 1994, 1995, 1996, 2000, 2001, 2002. Used by permission of NavPress Publishing Group."

Do you see why people are so confused? In its own words, this book claims to be:

- "A paraphrasing translation of the Bible"
- "The Bible in contemporary language"
- "A contemporary rendering of the Bible from the original languages"
- "The Message Bible"
- "Scripture"

Wow. It takes a lot of gall to call *The Message* "scripture." So-called "scholars" practically have a heart attack when we dare call the words of the King James Bible "scripture." But they will call *The Message* "scripture"? Unbelievable.

You've seen the evidence for yourself. There is no doubt. They are selling *The Message* as a Bible. So we will treat it like other Bible versions.

WHAT'S MISSING FROM "THE MESSAGE?"

As you have already seen, in some verses *The Message* uses many more words than God did. But other verses are missing all sorts of important details. Using the list of verses from Chapter 17, we can get a pretty good picture of what type of Greek text Peterson worked from.

Out of 257 potentially perverted verses, *The Message* is missing words and phrases in 208 of them, the same number as the Bible in Basic English and God's Word to the Nations, and just 9 less than Westcott and Hort's English ERV and American ASV Bibles.

In short, *The Message* is missing almost 81% of the words in our sample verses. That's not a paraphrase or translation. That's a *perversion* of the Bible.

Could it be an accident? I wondered too. Look at Mark 1:1:

King James Bible

> The beginning of the gospel of Jesus Christ, the Son of God;

The Message

> The good news of Jesus Christ--the Message!--begins here,

Anyone knows the words "the Son of God" are incredibly important. Yet "the Son of God" is missing from *The Message*.

The only two other English Bibles that even dared to remove "the Son of God" from Mark 1:1 were:

- The New World Translation (NWT) of the Jehovah's Witnesses
- Today's New International Version (TNIV)

But we can't generalize from just one verse. If you look at our list of 257 verses, you will see that, concerning the titles of the Lord Jesus Christ, *The Message* is missing:

- "Lord" in 11 verses: [120]
- "Jesus" in 7 verses: [121]
- "Christ" in 28 verses: [122]
- "Jesus" and "Christ" in 4 verses: [123]
- *Both* "Lord" and "Christ" in 4 verses: [124]
- Both "Lord" and "Jesus" in 2 Timothy 4:1.
- "Lord Jesus Christ" in 6 verses: [125]
- "God" in Matthew 6:33.
- "the Father, the Word and the Holy Ghost" in 1 John 5:7-8.

It's clear. It couldn't be a coincidence. It's not only missing the same words as other Alexandrian translations, it

---

120) Matthew 13:51; 28:6; Mark 9:24; Luke 9:57; 22:31; 23:42; Romans 6:11; 1 Corinthians 15:47; 2 Corinthians 4:10; Galatians 6:17 and 2 John 1:3.
121) Matthew 16:20; Acts 3:26; 1 Corinthians 5:5; 2 Corinthians 4:6; Colossians 1:28; 1 Timothy 1:1 and 1 Peter 5:10.
122) Matthew 23:8; Luke 4:41; John 4:42; Acts 2:30; 15:11; 16:31; 19:4; 20:21; Romans 1:16; 15:8; 1 Corinthians 5:4 (twice); 9:1, 18; 16:23; 2 Corinthians 11:31; Galatians 3:17; 4:7; Philippians 4:13; 1 Thessalonians 2:19; 3:11, 13; 1 Timothy 2:7; Hebrews 3:1; 1 John 1:7; 4:3; Revelation 1:9; 12:17 and 22:21.
123) 1 Corinthians 16:22; 2 Corinthians 5:18; Galatians 6:15 and Ephesians 3:9.
124) Romans 16:20; 2 Thessalonians 1:12; 1 Timothy 5:21 and Titus 1:4.
125) Romans 16:24; Ephesians 3:14; Colossians 1:2; 2 Thessalonians 1:8; 1 Timothy 1:1 and 2 Timothy 4:22.

even removed titles for the Son of God that are found in every Greek text in the world—including Alexandrian! [126]

As you will see from Chapter 17, it's missing a lot of other important words, too, just like the other Alexandrian Bibles. And that is exactly what *The Message* is: just another Alexandrian Bible.

If you want to send people the *right message*, give them the King James Bible instead. They need the whole truth of God, not the creative paraphrases of man.

---

126) See the footnotes regarding the MSG (The Message Bible) in Chapter 17.

15

THE BIBLE THAT ALMOST WAS

- **The Holman Christian Standard Bible (CSB)**

A THIRD FOUNDATION

If you want to build a house, the first thing you have to think about is your foundation. If your foundation is lousy, the rest of the house will not matter.

You can have the finest architects design it. You can use the most precious and expensive materials. You can decorate it any way you want. You can make it pretty or practical, and any style or shape you desire. But your house will never be any better than its foundation.

Throughout this book I have been telling you about two foundations: God's words preserved through history by faithful believers starting in Antioch of Syria;[127] and

---

127) These faithful believers are first mentioned in Acts 11:19-26. Paul and Barnabas were sent as missionaries from the church at Antioch in Acts 13:1-4.

man's perverted words from Alexandria, Egypt by way of Rome.[128]

But believe it or not, Brothers and Sisters, men have made up a third foundation.

Have you ever witnessed to someone, and given him the facts from reliable sources, including ones he himself trusts, and then he tries to squirm out of them? The fact is, he doesn't want to admit that he's wrong and you're right. That would mean that years of study or work or belief were all wrong. Nobody likes to feel like that.

What does he do? He doesn't want to accept the truth as you gave it to him, but he sees plainly that his belief doesn't hold water, either. So he invents a *third way*. Now he can leave his belief behind and still not accept yours.

A few textual scholars did that same thing. They could see that the vast majority of manuscripts read like the King James. And it was plainly obvious that the Egyptian manuscripts were hopelessly corrupt —you can't even find any two Alexandrian Bibles that agree with each other. But they didn't want to go "all the way" and accept the King James as God's preserved words in English, either.

What's a textual scholar to do? He's got years of work with manuscripts. And he doesn't want to feel they were all worthless. I'll tell you what he did. He came up with a third view, that isn't completely Preserved and isn't completely Alexandrian. How wishy-washy can you get, Charlie Brown?

---

128) For more about the history these "two streams" of manuscripts in an easy-to-read format, see *Did the Catholic Church Give us the Bible?* (2005). Available from Chick Publications.

Their third text was named, "The Majority Text." It's a made-up name, obviously. But it's also a made up text. It has never existed as a single volume, any more than there's some single book called "The Alexandrian Text" lying around somewhere. It's just another theory by "scholars" about a book that *never existed.*

THE SO-CALLED "MAJORITY TEXT" [129]

This so-called "Majority Text" adds to or takes away from about a third as many words as various Alexandrian-type Greek texts do. But that is still over 1,000 places in the New Testament.

Changing God's words is changing God's words, no matter how many times they do it. I don't want to face the fierce anger of Lord Jesus on Judgment Day, with the lame excuse that I "only" took away from His words one third as many times as the other guys. "Ye shall not add to or take away from," He said.

Some people tried to make their "Majority Text" fly anyway. In 1982 two men, Arthur Farstad and Zane Hodges, created a *Greek New Testament According to the Majority Text.* It's the Greek that's used in the *NKJV Greek-English Interlinear New Testament.* And it's basically that "M" you see in the footnotes of a New King James New Testament.

But the so-called "Majority Text" hadn't been translated into English. So in 1984 Arthur Farstad, who had been General Editor for the New King James Version, got the

---

129) For more information on the so-called "Majority Text", see *Answers to Your Bible Version Questions* (2003), pp. 110-111, 180-181 and 207. Available from Chick Publications.

idea to make an English New Testament based solely on his "Majority Text." He got some help from another scholar friend, Edwin Blum, but the project never got finished.

Jump ahead 14 years to 1998. Broadman & Holman, publishers for the Southern Baptists, were having a big problem. They needed a Bible to publish and use for scripture quotation, study Bibles and other projects.

They tried to buy the New American Standard but twice the deal fell through.

They thought about the NIV, but Zondervan, copyright holder to the NIV and Broadman & Holman, are rivals. Zondervan said they'd have to know about any of their rival's projects as a condition to using the NIV. Forget that idea.

Besides, this was about the time people started talking about a "gender neutral" NIV,[130] and that went over like a lead balloon. So both the NAS and NIV were out.

Finally, Broadman & Holman decided they'd make their own Bible. They knew Arthur Farstad already had experience being a general editor, so they offered him the job.

But Farstad wanted the New Testament based on his "Majority Text." So they offered a compromise.

They would pay for Farstad to finish his so-called "Majority Text" translation and give him a digital copy for his own use. In exchange, he would use instead the Alexandrian "critical" text for Holman's New Testament and let someone else handle the Old Testament. Farstad agreed. The Holman Christian Standard Bible was born.

---

130) See Chapter 11 about the "gender-neutral" NIV controversy.

Then five months into the project, Farstad died. [131] And that was the end of the Majority Text in English.

THE FAULTY FOUNDATION FOR THE CSB

Edwin Blum, Farstad's friend, became the General Editor, and the project went forward using the very "newest" critical Hebrew text for the Old Testament and "newest" critical Greek text for the New Testament. That became their foundation.

Upon that foundation they built, using a 78-person team of the finest translators, linguists, stylists and text-critical scholars. They used "the latest research in textual criticism along with sophisticated computer technology."

Like the NIV, the team came:

> "...from 20 denominations, including Southern Baptists, Plymouth Brethren, Presbyterians (PCA), Congregationalists, Church of England, Church of God, Evangelical Free Church, Methodists, Evangelical Mennonites and Episcopalians." [132]

They decorated their version with twice as many textual notes, explanations and special bullets to aid the reader.

They designed their Bible to be more literal than the NIV and NLT, less literal than the NAS, NAU and ESV, and less politically-correct than the TNIV or NRS.

---

131) The early story of the Holman CSB is largely based on a December 19, 2007 "Interview with Dr. Ed Blum, General Editor for the HCSB," by Will Lee, available on the internet. One important section of Blum's interview can be read at http://www.bible-researcher.com/csb.html.
132) See "Broadman & Holman Publishers announces new Bible translation" by John Perry, posted May 7, 1999 on Baptist Press news, at www.bpnews.net.

They even finished off their version with the claim that it rejected both "formal equivalence" and "dynamic equivalence" in translation, and used a third method, "optimal equivalence" —a balance between the two, according to them.

But you know what? None of that great-sounding stuff really matters. The Holman Christian Standard was built upon the faulty foundation of "textual criticism," just like almost every other "modern" Bible version.

Out of our 257 selected verses, the CSB is missing words, phrases and whole verses in 234 of them, the same number as the ESV and NET Bibles, just 3 less than the New World Translation of the Jehovah's Witnesses and 17 more than Westcott & Hort's ERV and ASV.

So in the end, there's not more than a few handfuls of difference between any of them. Faulty foundation, faulty Bible. Need I say more?

WHAT'S MISSING FROM THE HOLMAN CHRISTIAN STANDARD?

Just to make it clear, the Holman CSB is missing 91% of the words, phrases and verses listed in Chapter 17. That puts it in a three-way tie for 6th worst. [133]

Remember what I said about the CSB in Chapter 4:

> In a few places in the NT, large square brackets indicate texts that the HCSB translation team and most biblical scholars today believe were not part of the original text. However,

---

133) For the full list of worst to least bad Bibles, see the charts following Chapter 17.

these texts have been retained in brackets in the HCSB because of their undeniable antiquity and their value for tradition and the history of NT interpretation in the church.[134]

Just like the others, the CSB translators didn't believe those words, phrases and whole verses, but they put them in their text so you would buy their Bible. How can this many "scholars" and writers, for so many Bible versions, be this disbelieving and dishonest?

At least the *dis*believing translators of the Revised Standard, Revised English Bible, Jerusalem Bible, New Jerusalem and a few others didn't stoop to playing the italics and brackets games. They had the guts just to omit those words of God entirely. They didn't put them in the Bible with appeals to "undeniable antiquity" or "value for tradition." It hurt their sales. But at least they were honest.

- The translators of the CSB used brackets on 46 of our 257 selected verses, meaning they disbelieved them but stuck them in their Bible anyway:[135]

- Of the 45 whole verses marked as not belonging in the Bible in at least one version (see Chapter 17), the CSB bracketed 40 of them and removed one, 91% of our list of removed verses.

- The CSB removed Acts 15:34, "Notwithstanding it pleased Silas to abide there still," without any textual note whatsoever.

---

134) The *CSB Red-Letter Text Edition Bible* (2004), p. ix.
135) Matthew 17:21; 18:11; 21:44; 23:14; Mark 9:44, 46; 11:26; 15:28; 16:9-20; Luke 22:43-44; 23:17; John 5:4; 7:53-8:11; Acts 8:37; 24:7; 28:29; Romans 16:24.

- The CSB completely removed at least one of the words that Christ spoke in no less than 53 verses[136]

We don't need another Bible translation. We need to believe the one we have, that God preserved for us in the English language: the King James Bible.

All these other Bibles, including the 40 analyzed in this book, add to or take away from God's holy words in hundreds, even thousands of places. Many of these words added or removed are very subtle. But these translators are violating God's command, whether they add or remove many or few.

There is the old story of the well-off man who walked up to a pretty woman one evening. After a lot of small talk, he came to the point:

> "Would you sleep with me for a million dollars?"

The woman thought for a minute, then said, "Sure."

The man, not missing a beat, pulled out a $10 bill and said, "Let's go."

The woman was both astonished and angry. She scowled, "Not on your life. What kind of woman do you think I am?"

The man replied:

> "I already know what kind of woman you are. We are just negotiating the price."

---

136) Matthew 5:22, 44; 9:13; 12:35; 15:6, 8; 16:3, 20; 19:9, 17; 20:7, 16, 22; 22:30; 23:8; 24:7; 25:13, 31; 26:28; Mark 2:17; 4:11; 6:11; 8:26; 9:49; 10:21, 24; 12:30; 13:14, 33; 14:24; Luke 4:4, 8, 18; 9:55-56; 11:2, 4, 11, 29; 20:23; 21:4; 22:68; John 3:13, 15, 16, 18; 6:47; 16:10, 16; 17:12; Revelation 1:8, 11; 2:15.

When people, even well-meaning Bible translators, produce compromised Bibles, it does not matter how many words they added or took away.

We already know what they are. The only difference is how many words of God they did it to.

16

HOW MUCH SCRIPTURE ARE WE ALLOWED TO DOUBT?

What if a person believed every single scripture of the Bible, except those few that say Jesus Christ is the only way to heaven? Let's say we came up with 10 verses that clearly state or imply that.

There are 31,103 verses in the Bible. 10 out of 31,103 is only .03% —not a very high number. But think about the words of 2 John 1:9-11:

> Whosoever transgresseth, and abideth not in the doctrine of Christ, hath not God. He that abideth in the doctrine of Christ, he hath both the Father and the Son. If there come any unto you, and bring not this doctrine, receive him not into your house, neither bid him God speed: For he that biddeth him God speed is partaker of his evil deeds.

To transgress is to cross the line, to go too far. One Christian writer said abiding in the doctrine of Christ is like being on the very top of a mountain. One step back or one step forward, and you're not on the top anymore. You are either "abiding in the doctrine of Christ" or you are not. You either "have God" or you "do not have God." It's that simple.

You cannot play percentages with God's words. You either believe them all or you don't. You are either abiding in the doctrine of Christ, or you are not.

It doesn't say you have to understand them all. It means you have to believe them —trust that God is true and He knows what He said. Our Christian life is based on faith, not on doubt.

In 1983, while my future wife and I trained with the Summer Institute of Linguistics for Wycliffe Bible Translators, I read a quotation from Martin Luther. It was so powerful that it has influenced my thinking to this day:

> "If I profess with loudest voice and clearest exposition every portion of the truth of God except precisely that little point which the world and the devil are at the moment attacking, I am not confessing Christ, however boldly I may be professing Christ.
>
> Where the battle rages, there the loyalty of the soldier is proved, and to be steady on all the battlefield besides, is merely flight and disgrace if he flinches at that point."

You cannot pick and choose which scriptures you will believe and which ones you will doubt. There is a battle going on, and at stake is the eternal destiny of every person on earth. They are either going to heaven, to be forever with our Heavenly Father, or they are going straight to hell, and after a horrifying judgment to the lake of fire.

Which Bible they read, and what they believe, makes all the difference in the world —this one and the next.

When they ask you "Which Bible?" I pray you know exactly what to say, without doubting.

May God bless you as you make the right choice.

PART THREE

WHAT'S MISSING FROM YOUR BIBLE?

17

LOOK WHAT'S MISSING ...
IN 40 VERSIONS

The following selection of 257 verses is just a small selection of the many words, phrases or whole verses missing in 40 commonly used Bibles. Remember, the true and preserved Bible won't be missing *any* of them.

THE SHORT LIST:
45 MISSING VERSES IN MODERN BIBLES

Out of the 257 verses covered in this chapter, 45 verses are missing in at least one Bible version. They indicate this by italicizing, bracketing, setting apart the verses, or removing them altogether.

Below are several verses quoted from the King James Bible. The lined-out text has been removed from the Bible versions listed below each verse:

(Matthew 16:2-3) He answered and said unto them, ~~When it is evening, ye say,~~ *It will be* ~~fair weather: for the sky is red. And in the morning,~~ *It will be* ~~foul weather to day: for the sky is red and lowring. O~~ *ye* ~~hypocrites, ye can discern the face of the sky; but can ye not~~ *discern* ~~the signs of the times?~~

Missing from: *AMP,* MOF, NEB, REB

* See Chapter 6 for more about these verses.

❧ ❧ ❧

(Matthew 17:21) ~~Howbeit this kind goeth not out but by prayer and fasting.~~

Missing from: *AMP, ASV,* Bar, BBE, CJB, [CSB], ERV, ICB, JB, MOF, NAB, [NAS], [NAU], NCV, NEB, NET, NIrV, NIV, NJB, NLT, NRS, NWT, Phi, REB, RSV, TNIV

❧ ❧ ❧

(Matthew 18:11) ~~For the Son of man is come to save that which was lost.~~

Missing from: *AMP, ASV,* Bar, BBE, CEV, CJB, [CSB], ERV, ESV, GNB, GWN, ICB, JB, *MRC,* MOF, MSG, NAB, [NAS], [NAU], NCV, NEB, NET, NIrV, NIV, NJB, NLT, NRS, NWT, Phi, RSV, TNIV, WNT

❧ ❧ ❧

(Matthew 21:44) ~~And whosoever shall fall on this stone shall be broken: but on whomsoever it shall fall, it will grind him to powder.~~

Missing from: *AMP,* CJB, [CSB], GNB, JB, (NAB), NEB, NIV, NJB, NRS, (Phi), REB, RSV

❧ ❧ ❧

Matthew 23:14 ~~Woe unto you, scribes and Pharisees, hypocrites! for ye devour widows' houses, and for a pretence make long prayer: therefore ye shall receive the greater damnation.~~

Missing from: *AMP*, *ASV*, Bar, BBE, CEV, CJB, [CSB], DBY, ERV, ESV, GNB, *ISV*, GWN, ICB, JB, *MRC*, MOF, MSG, NAB, [NAS], [NAU], NCV, NEB, NET, NIrV, NIV, NJB, NLT, NRS, NWT, Phi, REB, RSV, TNIV, WNT

ഔ ഔ ഔ

Mark 7:16 ~~If any man have ears to hear, let him hear.~~

Missing from: *AMP*, *ASV*, Bar, BBE, CEV, CJB, ERV, ESV, GNB, ICB, LB, *MRC*, MSG, NAB, [NAS], [NAU], NCV, NEB, NET, NIrV, NIV, NLT, NRS, NWT, Phi, REB, RSV, TNIV, WNT

ഔ ഔ ഔ

Mark 9:44 ~~Where their worm dieth not, and the fire is not quenched.~~

Missing from: AMP, *ASV*, Bar, BBE, CEV, CJB, [CSB], DBY, ERV, ESV, GNB, GWN, ICB, JB, LB, MOF, *MRC*, MSG, NAB, [NAS], [NAU], NCV, NEB, NET, NIrV, NIV, NJB, NLT, NRS, NWT, Phi, REB, RSV, TNIV, WNT

ഔ ഔ ഔ

Mark 9:46 ~~Where their worm dieth not, and the fire is not quenched.~~

Missing from: AMP, *ASV*, Bar, BBE, CEV, CJB, [CSB], DBY, ERV, ESV, GNB, GWN, ICB, JB, LB, MOF, *MRC*, MSG, NAB, [NAS], [NAU], NCV, NEB, NET, NIrV, NIV, NJB, NLT, NRS, NWT, Phi, REB, RSV, TNIV, WNT

ഔ ഔ ഔ

Mark 11:26 ~~But if ye do not forgive, neither will your Father which is in heaven forgive your trespasses.~~

Missing from: *AMP*, *ASV*, Bar, BBE, CEV, CJB, [CSB], ERV, ESV, GNB, GWN, ICB, JB, LB, MOF, *MRC*, MSG, NAB, [NAS], [NAU], NCV, NEB, NET, NIrV, NIV, NJB, NLT, NRS, NWT, Phi, REB, RSV, TNIV, WNT

৯৹   ৯৹   ৯৹

Mark 15:28 ~~And the scripture was fulfilled, which saith, And he was numbered with the transgressors.~~

Missing from: *AMP*, *ASV*, Bar, BBE, CEV, CJB, [CSB], *DBY*, ERV, ESV, GNB, GWN, ICB, ISV, JB, MOF, *MRC*, MSG, NAB, [NAS], [NAU], NCV, NEB, NET, NIrV, NIV, NJB, NLT, NRS, NWT, Phi, REB, RSV, TNIV, WNT

৯৹   ৯৹   ৯৹

Mark 16:9-20 ~~Now when *Jesus* was risen early the first day of the week, he appeared first to Mary Magdalene, out of whom he had cast seven devils. *And* she went and told them that had been with him, as they mourned and wept. And they, when they had heard that he was alive, and had been seen of her, believed not. After that he appeared in another form unto two of them, as they walked, and went into the country. And they went and told *it* unto the residue: neither believed they them. Afterward he appeared unto the eleven as they sat at meat, and upbraided them with their unbelief and hard-~~

ness of heart, because they believed not them which had seen him after he was risen. And he said unto them, Go ye into all the world, and preach the gospel to every creature. He that believeth and is baptized shall be saved; but he that believeth not shall be damned. And these signs shall follow them that believe; In my name shall they cast out devils; they shall speak with new tongues; They shall take up serpents; and if they drink any deadly thing, it shall not hurt them; they shall lay hands on the sick, and they shall recover. So then after the Lord had spoken unto them, he was received up into heaven, and sat on the right hand of God. And they went forth, and preached every where, the Lord working with *them*, and confirming the word with signs following. Amen.

Missing from: _ASV, _Bar, _CEV⟨137⟩ [CSB], ERV, [ESV], [GNB], (MOF)⟨138⟩ MRC, [MSG], (NAB), [NAS], [NAU], [NCV], [NET], |NIrV⟨139⟩ |NIV,

---

137) The CEV labels these verses "One Old Ending to Mark's Gospel" and added the other (fake) ending as well, labeled "Another Old Ending to Mark's Gospel."
138) Moffatt (MOF) called verses 9-20 ending "(a)," but between verses 14-15 stuck in a totally *different* verse that came from Codex W. Then he added a second ending (b), with another verse someone added.
139) In "A Word about the NIrV," it says "Later copies of the Greek New Testament added several verses that the earlier ones don't have. Sometimes it's several verses in a row. When that's the case, we included them in the NIrV. But we set those verses off with a long line. That tells you that the first writers didn't write them. They were added later on." But if they don't believe they belong, *why put them in their Bible?* Because they still want you to buy their Bible.

ORIGINAL END IS 'LOST'?

_NLT, [[NRS]], |NWT⁽¹⁴⁰⁾ _Phi⁽¹⁴¹⁾ RSV, |TNIV, [WNT]

The following Bibles have Mark 16:9-20 *in the text*. But I have listed them separately with a raised F (ᶠ) because they also have a *footnote* that causes the reader to doubt that these 12 verses are truly scripture:

Missing from: AMP ᶠ, BBE ᶠ ⑴⁴²⁾ CJB ᶠ, GWN ᶠ, ICB ᶠ, ISV ᶠ, JB ᶠ, LB ᶠ, NEB ᶠ, NJB ᶠ, REB ᶠ

🙠 🙠 🙠

Luke 22:43 And there appeared an angel unto him from heaven, strengthening him.

Missing from: [CSB], (NAB), Phi, RSV

🙠 🙠 🙠

Luke 22:44 And being in an agony he prayed more earnestly: and his sweat was as it were great drops of blood falling down to the ground.

Missing from: [CSB], (NAB), Phi, RSV

🙠 🙠 🙠

Luke 23:17 (For of necessity he must release one unto them at the feast.)

Missing from: *AMP*, *ASV*, Bar, BBE, CEV, CJB, [CSB], ERV, ESV, GNB, GWN, ICB, JB, LB, MOF, *MRC*, MSG, NAB, [NAS], [NAU], NCV, NEB,

---

140) The NWT labels verses 9-20 the "Long Conclusion," writing this disclaimer: "Certain ancient manuscripts (A C D) and versions (Vg Sy^{c,p}) add the following long conclusion, but which א B Sy^s Arm omit."

141) Verses 9-20 appear in the JB Phillips (Phi) text, but they are set apart with this label: "*An Ancient Appendix*." Clearly he did not believe these were the words of God (yet he put them in his Bible).

142) The BBE is way more subtle than most. It writes 16:8 as if it were broken off mid-sentence, ending the verse like this: "because they were full of fear that…" as if the original ending was lost. And that's what many teach in Bible colleges today.

NET, NIrV, NIV, NJB, NLT, NRS, NWT, Phi, REB, RSV, TNIV, WNT

❧   ❧   ❧

Luke 24:12 ~~Then arose Peter, and ran unto the sepulchre; and stooping down, he beheld the linen clothes laid by themselves, and departed, wondering in himself at that which was come to pass.~~

Missing from: *MRC*, [NAS], NEB, [[NWT]], REB, RSV

❧   ❧   ❧

Luke 24:40 ~~And when he had thus spoken, he shewed them his hands and his feet.~~

Missing from: Bar, *MRC*, [NAS], NEB, [[NWT]], Phi, REB, RSV

❧   ❧   ❧

John 5:4 ~~For an angel went down at a certain season into the pool, and troubled the water: whosoever then first after the troubling of the water stepped in was made whole of whatsoever disease he had.~~

Missing from: *AMP*, Bar, ASV, BBE, CEV, CJB, [CSB], *DBY*, ERV, ESV, GNB, GWN, ICB, (LB), [MOF], MSG, NAB, [NAS], [NAU], NCV, NEB, NET, NIrV, NIV, NJB, NLT, NRS, NWT, (Phi), REB, RSV, TNIV, WNT

❧   ❧   ❧

John 7:53-8:11 ~~And every man went unto his own house. Jesus went unto the mount of Olives. And early in the morning he came again into the temple, and all the people came unto him; and he sat down, and taught~~

THESE VERSES HAVE NO FIXED PLACE IN SCRIPTURE?

~~them. And the scribes and Pharisees brought unto him a woman taken in adultery; and when they had set her in the midst, They say unto him, Master, this woman was taken in adultery, in the very act. Now Moses in the law commanded us, that such should be stoned: but what sayest thou? This they said, tempting him, that they might have to accuse him. But Jesus stooped down, and with his finger wrote on the ground,~~ *as though he heard them not.* ~~So when they continued asking him, he lifted up himself, and said unto them, He that is without sin among you, let him first cast a stone at her. And again he stooped down, and wrote on the ground. And they which heard~~ *it*, ~~being convicted by~~ *their own* ~~conscience, went out one by one, beginning at the eldest,~~ *even* ~~unto the last: and Jesus was left alone, and the woman standing in the midst. When Jesus had lifted up himself, and saw none but the woman, he said unto her, Woman, where are those thine accusers? hath no man condemned thee? She said, No man, Lord. And Jesus said unto her, Neither do I condemn thee: go, and sin no more.~~

Missing from: [ASV], *BBE*, [CSB], [ERV], [[ESV]], [GNB], [MOF], *MRC*, [NAS], [NAU], |NCV, NEB⁽¹⁴³⁾ [NET], |NIrV, |NIV, _NLT, [[NRS]], |NWT, REB, RSV, |TNIV, [WNT]

---

143) The NEB and REB print this at the end of John, in a separate section, with a note both at 7:53 and the end of John, saying it "has no fixed place" in the gospel.

The following Bibles have John 7:53-8:11 *in the text*. But I have listed them separately with a double raised-F (FF) because they also have a footnote that causes the reader to doubt that these 12 verses are truly scripture:

Missing from: AMP FF, Bar FF, Phi FF, CEV FF, CJB FF, GWN FF, ICB FF, ISV FF, JB FF, LB FF, NJB FF

လွ   လွ   လွ

Acts 8:37 And Philip said, If thou believest with all thine heart, thou mayest. And he answered and said, I believe that Jesus Christ is the Son of God.

Missing from: AMP, ASV, Bar, BBE, CEV, CJB, [CSB], DBY, ERV, ESV, GNB, GWN, HNV, ICB, ISV, JB, MOF, MRC, MSG, NAB, [NAS], [NAU], NCV, NEB, NET, NIrV, NIV, NJB, NLT, NRS, NWT, Phi, REB, RSV, TNIV, WNT

လွ   လွ   လွ

Acts 15:34 Notwithstanding it pleased Silas to abide there still.

Missing from: AMP, ASV, Bar, BBE, CEV, CJB, CSB, DBY, ERV, ESV, GNB, GWN, ICB, ISV, JB, LB, MOF, MRC, MSG, NAB, [NAS], [NAU], NCV, NEB, NET, NIrV, NIV, NJB, NLT, NRS, NWT, Phi, REB, RSV, TNIV, WNT

လွ   လွ   လွ

Acts 24:7 But the chief captain Lysias came upon us, and with great violence took him away out of our hands,

Missing from: AMP, ASV, Bar, BBE, CEV, CJB, [CSB], DBY, ERV, ESV, GNB, GWN, HNV, ICB, ISV, MOF, MRC, MSG, NAB, [NAS], [NAU], NCV, NEB, NIrV, NIV, NJB, NLT, NRS, NWT, Phi, REB, RSV, TNIV, WNT

❧   ❧   ❧

(Acts 28:29) ~~And when he had said these words, the Jews departed, and had great reasoning among themselves~~.

Missing from: *AMP*, *ASV*, Bar, BBE, CEV, CJB, [CSB], DBY, ERV, ESV, GNB, GWN, ICB, *ISV*, JB, LB, MOF, *MRC*, MSG, NAB, [NAS], [NAU], NCV, NEB, NET, NIrV, NIV, NJB, NLT, NRS, NWT, Phi, REB, RSV, TNIV, WNT

❧   ❧   ❧

Romans 16:24 ~~The grace of our Lord Jesus Christ *be* with you all. Amen~~.

Missing from: *AMP*, *ASV*, Bar, BBE, CEV, CJB, [CSB], ERV, ESV, GNB, GWN, ICB, *ISV*, JB, MOF, *MRC*, MSG, NAB, [NAS], [NAU], NCV, NEB, NET, NIrV, NIV, NLT, NRS, NWT, Phi, REB, RSV, TNIV, WNT

THE BIG LIST:
257 VERSES MISSING TEXT IN MODERN BIBLES

MISSING TITLES OF THE LORD JESUS CHRIST

The Alexandrians and other doubters of God and His words had a special interest in shaving off the titles of God's Son. We humans are fickle. The less something or someone is mentioned, the quicker we forget. And the less we see the three main titles of the Son of God, the quicker our understanding of Him falls to pieces. DANG!

What are the three main titles, and what do they mean?

(LORD) means two things:

1. Jesus Christ is Lord, as in the Master or Boss of everything.

2. Jesus Christ is Lord, which is another way of acknowledging Him as God Himself. When the New Testament quotes the covenant name of God[144] out of the Old Testament, it uses this word.

JESUS is the human name of God (also known as "Emmanuel"—God with us) who became an actual man in history.

CHRIST is the Greek term for the Messiah, the One who fulfilled all of the Old Testament prophecies for a coming deliverer and Saviour of Israel, and ultimately of the whole world.

All three of these titles are important. In fact, the phrase "Lord Jesus Christ" occurs in 81 New Testament verses. Notice below that over and over again, one or more titles of God the Son are *missing* from Alexandrian-tainted Bibles.

WHAT'S MISSING: LORD *P. 147-153*

Matthew 13:51 Jesus saith unto them, Have ye understood all these things? They say unto him, Yea, ~~Lord~~.

Missing from: *AMP*, ASV, Bar, BBE, CEV, CJB, CSB, *DBY*, DRA, ERV, ESV, GNB, GWN, ICB, ISV, JB, LB, MRC, MSG, MOF, NAB, NAS, NAU, NEB, NET, NCV, NIrV, NIV, NJB, NLT, NWT, NRS, Phi, REB, RSV, TCW, TNIV, WNT

YAHWEH

144) This is the name, Jehovah, or JHVH, or YHWH, capitalized LORD in most Bibles.

JESUS ISNT LORD?!

ൢ   ൢ   ൢ

(Matthew 28:6) He is not here: for he is risen, as he said. Come, see the place where ~~the Lord~~ lay.

Missing from: AMP, Bar, CEV, CJB, CSB, ESV, GNB, GWN, ICB, ISV, JB, LB, MRC, MSG, NAB, NAS, NAU, NCV, NEB, NET, NIrV, NIV, NJB, NLT, NRS, NWT, Phi, REB, RSV, TCW, TNIV, WNT

ൢ   ൢ   ൢ

(Mark 9:24) And straightway the father of the child cried out, and said with tears, ~~Lord~~, I believe; help thou mine unbelief.

Here they removed the father's simply expressed faith in the Lord Jesus.

Missing from: ASV, Bar, BBE, CEV, CJB, CSB, DBY, ERV, ESV, GNB, GWN, HNV, ICB, ISV, JB, LB, MOF, MRC, MSG, NAB, NAS, NAU, NCV, NEB, NET, NIrV, NIV, NJB, NLT, NRS, NWT, Phi, REB, RSV, TCW(145) TNIV, WEB, WNT

ൢ   ൢ   ൢ

(Luke 9:57) And it came to pass, that, as they went in the way, a certain man said unto him, ~~Lord~~, I will follow thee whithersoever thou goest.

There is a big difference between being willing to follow an ordinary man around and following the Lord anywhere He goes. One is simply a personal pledge or political preference. The other is a life-long decision.

Missing from: AMP, ASV, Bar, BBE, CEV, CJB, CSB,

---

145) TCW strangely removes "Lord" and adds instead, "Teacher" —a word found in *no* Greek manuscript, anywhere.

WHAT?

DRA, ERV, ESV, GNB, GWN, ICB, ISV, JB, LB, MOF, MRC, MSG, NAB, NAS, NAU, NCV, NEB, NET, NIrV, NIV, NJB, NLT, NRS, NWT, Phi, REB, RSV, TNIV, WNT

൭   ൭   ൭

(Luke 17:6) And ~~the Lord~~ said, If ye had faith as a grain of mustard seed, ye might say unto this sycamine tree, Be thou plucked up by the root, and be thou planted in the sea; and it should obey you.

Why is this missing in these versions? It's in *every* Greek manuscript. What kind of translator would take away God's words, when everyone knows they belong there?

Missing from: CEV, LB, NIrV, NIV, Phi, TCW[146] TNIV

൭   ൭   ൭

(Luke 22:31) ~~And the Lord said~~, Simon, Simon, behold, Satan hath desired to have you, that he may sift you as wheat:

Missing from: AMP, ASV, Bar, BBE, CEV[147] CJB, CSB, ERV, ESV, GNB, *GWN*, ICB, ISV, JB, LB, MOF, MRC, MSG, NAB, NAS, NAU, NEB, NET, NIrV, NIV, NJB, NLT, NRS, NWT, Phi, REB, RSV, TCW, TNIV, WNT

൭   ൭   ൭

(Luke 23:42) And he said ~~unto~~ Jesus, ~~Lord~~, remember me when thou comest into thy kingdom.

---

146) TCW removes "the Lord" and adds "Jesus," ~~found in~~ *no* Greek manuscript, anywhere.

147) The CEV and TCW remove "the Lord" and add "Jesus," found in *no* Greek manuscript.

It was clear to the thief who was on the cross next to Him. Obviously he couldn't merely call Him "Jesus" once he realized He was the King, about to enter into His heavenly kingdom.

Missing from: *AMP*, ASV, Bar, BBE, CEV, CJB, CSB, *DBY*, ERV, ESV, GNB, GWN, ICB, ISV, JB, LB, MOF, MRC, MSG, NAB, NAS, NAU, NCV, NEB, NET, NIrV, NIV, NJB, NLT, NRS, NWT, Phi, REB, RSV, WNT

ɷ ɷ ɷ

Romans 6:11 Likewise reckon ye also yourselves to be dead indeed unto sin, but alive unto God through Jesus Christ ~~our Lord~~.

Missing from: AMP, ASV, Bar[148] BBE, CEV, CJB, CSB, DBY, ERV, ESV, GNB, GWN, ICB, ISV, JB, MRC, MSG, NAB, NAS, NAU, NCV, NEB, NET, NIrV, NIV, NJB, NLT, NRS, NWT, REB, RSV, TCW, TNIV, WNT

ɷ ɷ ɷ

1 Corinthians 15:47 The first man is of the earth, earthy: the second man is ~~the Lord~~ from heaven.

This is not just any "heavenly man." The missing words prove this is "the Lord," God the Son Himself, Jesus Christ.

Missing from: *AMP*, ASV, Bar, BBE, CEV, CJB, CSB, DBY, DRA, ERV, ESV, GNB, GWN, ICB, ISV, JB, LB, MOF, MRC, MSG[149] NAB, NAS, NAU, NCV, NEB, NET, NIrV, NIV, NJB, NLT, NRS, NWT, Phi, REB, RSV, TCW[150] TNIV, WNT

---

148) Barclay also took away "through Jesus Christ," though every Greek text has it.
149) The MSG changes the whole meaning of this verse and says "a firm base shaped from the earth, a final completion coming out of heaven."
150) TCW completely rewrites this verse. It has almost *nothing* in common with the real words.

❧   ❧   ❧

2 Corinthians 4:10 Always bearing about in the body the dying of ~~the Lord~~ Jesus, that the life also of Jesus might be made manifest in our body.

Missing from: *AMP*, ASV, Bar, BBE, CEV, CJB, CSB, DBY, DRA, ERV, ESV, GNB, GWN, ICB, ISV, JB, LB, MOF, MRC, MSG, NAB, NAS, NAU, NCV, NEB, NET, NIrV, NIV, NJB, NLT, NRS, NWT, Phi, REB, RSV, TNIV, WNT

❧   ❧   ❧

Galatians 6:17 From henceforth let no man trouble me: for I bear in my body the marks of ~~the Lord~~ Jesus.

Missing from: ASV, Bar, BBE, CEV, CJB, CSB, ERV, ESV, GNB, GWN, ICB, ISV, JB, LB, MRC, MSG, NAB, NAS, NAU, NCV, NEB, NET, NIrV, NIV, NJB, NLT, NRS, NWT, Phi, REB, RSV, TCW, TNIV

❧   ❧   ❧

1 Timothy 1:1 Paul, an apostle of Jesus Christ by the commandment of God our Saviour, and ~~Lord~~ Jesus Christ, which is our hope;

Missing from: AMP, ASV, Bar, BBE, CEV, CJB, CSB, DBY, DRA, ERV, ESV, GNB, GWN, HNV, ICB, ISV, JB, MOF, MRC, MSG(151), NAB, NAS, NAU, NCV, NEB, NET, NIrV, NIV, NJB, NLT, NRS, NWT, Phi, REB, RSV, TCW, TNIV, WEB, WNT

❧   ❧   ❧

1 Timothy 5:21 I charge thee before God,

---

151) The MSG removes "Jesus" from "Jesus Christ" at the beginning, then removes the entire title, "Lord Jesus Christ". All that's left of God the Son in that verse is "Christ."

and the ~~Lord~~ Jesus Christ, and the elect angels, that thou observe these things without preferring one before another, doing nothing by partiality.

Missing from: AMP, ASV, Bar, BBE, CEV, CJB, CSB, DBY, DRA, ERV, ESV, GNB, GWN, HNV, ICB, ISV, JB, MRC, MSG[152] NAB, NAS, NAU, NCV, NEB, NET, NIrV, NIV, NJB, NLT, NRS, NWT, Phi, REB, RSV, TNIV, WEB, WNT

2 Timothy 4:1 I charge thee therefore before God, and ~~the Lord~~ Jesus Christ, who shall judge the quick and the dead at his appearing and his kingdom;

Missing from: AMP, ASV, Bar, BBE, CEV, CJB, CSB, DBY, DRA, ERV, ESV, GNB, GWN, ICB, ISV, JB, LB, MOF, MRC, MSG[153] NAB, NAS, NAU, NCV, NEB, NET, NIrV, NIV, NJB, NLT, NRS, NWT, Phi, REB, RSV, TNIV, WNT

Titus 1:4 To Titus, mine own son after the common faith: Grace, mercy, and peace, from God the Father and the ~~Lord~~ Jesus Christ our Saviour.

Missing from: *AMP*, ASV, Bar, BBE, CEV, CJB, CSB, DBY, DRA, ERV, ESV, GNB, GWN, ICB, ISV, JB, LB, MOF, MRC, MSG[154] NAB, NAS, NAU, NCV, NEB, NET, NIrV, NIV, NJB, NLT, NRS, NWT, Phi, REB, RSV, TCW, TNIV, WNT

---

152) The MSG *butchers* this verse from "the Lord Jesus Christ, and the elect angels" down to "Jesus and angels".

153) The MSG not only removes "the Lord," but also "Jesus."

154) The MSG not only removes "Lord," but "Christ" as well.

(2 John 1:3) Grace be with you, mercy, and peace, ~~from~~ God the Father, and from ~~the Lord~~ Jesus Christ, the Son of the Father, in truth and love.

Missing from: AMP, ASV, Bar, BBE, CEV, CJB, CSB, DRA, ERV, ESV, GNB, GWN, ICB, ISV, JB, LB, MOF, MRC, MSG, NAB, NAS, NAU, NCV, NEB, NET, NIrV, NIV, NJB, NLT, NRS, NWT, REB, RSV, TNIV, WNT

WHAT'S MISSING? JESUS P. 153 - 156

Matthew 8:29 And, behold, they cried out, saying, What have we to do with thee, ~~Jesus~~, thou Son of God? art thou come hither to torment us before the time?

Missing from: *AMP*, ASV, Bar, BBE, CJB, CSB, DBY, ERV, ESV, GNB, GWN, ICB, ISV, JB, LB, MRC, MSG, MOF, NAB, NAS, NAU, NCV, NEB, NET, NIrV, NIV, NJB, NLT, NRS, NWT, Phi, REB, RSV, TCW, TNIV, WNT

જ જ જ

(Matthew 16:20) Then charged he his disciples that they should tell no man that he was ~~Jesus~~ the Christ.

Missing from: *AMP*, ASV, Bar, BBE, CEV, CJB, CSB, DBY, ERV, ESV, GNB, GWN, ICB, ISV, JB, LB, MRC, MOF, MSG, NAB, NAS, NAU, NCV, NEB, NET, NIrV, NIV, NJB, NLT, NRS, NWT, Phi, REB, RSV, TCW, TNIV, WNT

જ જ જ

(Matthew 17:22) And while they abode in Galilee, ~~Jesus~~ said unto them, The Son of man shall be betrayed into the hands of men:

[handwritten in left margin: OR IS HE THE SON A SERVANT?!]

[handwritten at bottom: IF JESUS ISNT GOD IN FLESH WHO IS?!]

What's going on? *Every* Greek manuscript has Jesus' name here. So why is it missing in these Bibles?

Missing from: NIV, TNIV

∾ ∾ ∾

Matthew 18:2 And ~~Jesus~~ called a little child unto him, and set him in the midst of them,

Missing from: AMP, ASV, BBE, CJB, CSB, ERV, ESV, GWN, ISV, JB, MRC, MOF, NAB, NAS, NAU, NEB, NET, NIV, NJB, NRS, REB, RSV, TCW, TNIV, WNT

∾ ∾ ∾

Mark 14:18 And as they sat and did eat, ~~Jesus~~ said, Verily I say unto you, One of you which eateth with me shall betray me.

Again, since every Greek manuscript includes the word "Jesus," and almost every Bible version, what possible reason could the translators have for taking it out of these versions?

Missing from: NIV, TNIV

∾ ∾ ∾

Acts 3:26 Unto you first God, having raised up his Son ~~Jesus~~, sent him to bless you, in turning away every one of you from his iniquities.

Not only is the word "Jesus" taken out, but most modern versions change "Son" to "servant"—hiding the fact that Jesus is God the Son.

Missing from: *AMP*, ASV, Bar[155] BBE, CEV, CJB,

---

155) Barclay (Bar) and the BBE are also missing the words "having raised up," (referring to Christ's resurrection), even though *every* Greek text has it.

NO RESURRECTION?!

CSB, DBY, DRA, ERV, ESV, GNB, GWN, ICB, ISV, JB, LB, MOF, MRC, MSG, NAB, NAS, NAU, NEB, NET, NIrV, NIV, NJB, NLT, NRS, NWT, Phi, REB, RSV, TNIV, WNT

૭૦ ૭૦ ૭૦

Romans 15:8 Now I say that ~~Jesus~~ Christ was a minister of the circumcision for the truth of God, to confirm the promises made unto the fathers:

Missing from: AMP, ASV, Bar, BBE, CEV, CJB, CSB, ERV, ESV, GNB, GWN, HNV, ICB, ISV, JB, MOF, MRC, MSG[156], NAB, NAS, NAU, NCV, NEB, NET, NIrV, NIV, NJB, NLT, NRS, NWT, Phi, REB, RSV, TCW, TNIV, WEB, WNT

૭૦ ૭૦ ૭૦

1 Corinthians 5:5 To deliver such an one unto Satan for the destruction of the flesh, that the spirit may be saved in the day of the Lord ~~Jesus~~.

Missing from: Bar, CJB, CSB, ESV, GNB, GWN, ICB, ISV, JB, MSG, NAB, NCV, NEB, NET, NIrV, NIV, NJB, NLT, NRS, NWT, REB, TCW[157], TNIV

૭૦ ૭૦ ૭૦

2 Corinthians 4:6 For God, who command-ed the light to shine out of darkness, hath shined in our hearts, to give the light of the knowledge of the glory of God in the face of ~~Jesus~~ Christ.

Missing from: *AMP, DBY,* ICB, GNB, GWN, JB,

---

156) The MSG does the opposite: unlike any Greek manuscript anywhere, it keeps "Jesus" and removes "Christ".
157) TCW perverted this verse so drastically that the only main words in common with the real Bible are "Satan" and "save(d)."

MOF, MRC, MSG, (NAB), NAS, NAU, NCV, NET, NIrV, NIV, NJB, NWT, Phi, RSV, TCW, TNIV, WNT

❧   ❧   ❧

2 Corinthians 5:18 And all things are of God, who hath reconciled us to himself by ~~Jesus~~ Christ, and hath given to us the ministry of reconciliation;

Missing from: *AMP*, ASV, Bar, BBE, CEV, CJB, CSB, *DBY*, DRA, ERV, ESV, GNB, GWN, ICB, ISV, JB, MOF, MRC, MSG⁵⁸ NAB, NAS, NAU, NCV, NEB, NET, NIrV, NIV, NJB, NLT, NRS, NWT, Phi, REB, RSV, TCW, TNIV, WNT

❧   ❧   ❧

Colossians 1:28 Whom we preach, warning every man, and teaching every man in all wisdom; that we may present every man perfect in Christ ~~Jesus~~:

Missing from: AMP, ASV, Bar, BBE, CEV, CJB, CSB, DBY, ERV, ESV, GNB, GWN, ICB, ISV, JB, LB, MOF, MRC, MSG, NAB, NAS, NAU, NCV, NEB, NET, NIrV, NIV, NJB, NLT, NRS, NWT, Phi, REB, RSV, TNIV, WNT

❧   ❧   ❧

1 Peter 5:10 But the God of all grace, who hath called us unto his eternal glory by Christ ~~Jesus~~, after that ye have suffered a while, make you perfect, stablish, strengthen, settle you.

Missing from: *AMP*, ASV, Bar, CJB, ERV, ESV, GNB, ICB, JB, LB, MRC, MSG, (NAB), NAS, NAU, NCV, NEB, NET, NIrV, NIV, NJB, NRS, NWT, Phi, REB, RSV, TCW, TNIV, WNT

---

158) The MSG removes both "Jesus" and "Christ," saying "God who settled the relationship between us and him," taking away Jesus Christ's role in salvation.

JESUS DOESN'T SAVE US ?!

WHAT'S MISSING? CHRIST P. 157-167

(Matthew 23:8) But be not ye called Rabbi: for one is your Master, even ~~Christ~~; and all ye are brethren.

Missing from: AMP, ASV, Bar, BBE, CEV, CJB, CSB, DBY, DRA, ERV, ESV, GNB, GWN, ISV, JB, LB[159] MRC, MOF, MSG, NAS, NAU, NCV, NEB, NET, NIrV, NIV, NLT, NRS, NWT, Phi, REB, RSV, TCW, TNIV, WNT

℘   ℘   ℘

(Luke 4:41) And devils also came out of many, crying out, and saying, Thou art ~~Christ~~ the Son of God. And he rebuking them suffered them not to speak: for they knew that he was Christ.

The following versions took out the part where the devils said Jesus was "Christ." How would anyone find out they "knew that he was Christ," unless they said so themselves? In the preserved Bibles, they did.

Missing from: AMP, ASV, Bar, BBE, CEV, CJB, CSB, DBY, DRA, ERV, ESV, GNB, GWN, ICB, ISV, JB, LB, MOF, MRC, MSG, NAB, NAS, NAU, NCV, NEB, NET, NIrV, NIV, NJB, NLT, NRS, NWT, Phi, RSV, TCW, TNIV, WNT

℘   ℘   ℘

(John 4:42) And said unto the woman, Now we believe, not because of thy saying: for we have heard him ourselves, and know that this is indeed ~~the Christ~~, the Saviour of the world.

Missing from: *AMP*, ASV, Bar, BBE, CEV, CJB, CSB,

JESUS ISN'T GOD?!

159) The LB takes away "Christ" and substitutes "God." But everyone knows God is our Master. The point is that *Jesus Christ* is our Master.

JESUS CHRIST NOT THE SAVIOR?!

DBY, DRA, ERV, ESV, GNB, GWN, ICB, ISV, JB,
LB, MOF, MRC, MSG, NAB, NAS, NAU, NCV,
NEB, NET, NIrV, NIV, NJB, NLT, NRS, NWT, Phi,
REB, RSV, TNIV, WNT

୨ଡ଼   ୨ଡ଼   ୨ଡ଼

Acts 2:30 Therefore being a prophet, and
knowing that God had sworn with an oath to
him, that of the fruit of his loins, ~~according
to the flesh, he would raise up Christ~~ to sit
on his throne;

It isn't a "prophecy" that one of David's descendants
would sit on his throne. That's called a "dynasty." Most
kings did that. But saying that one of his human descendants would be the Messiah, who would be raised from
the dead and would sit on his throne —now *that* was a
prophecy.

Why are these versions missing the words that make
sense out of this prophecy?

Missing from: AMP, ASV, Bar, BBE, CEV, CJB, CSB,
DBY, DRA, ERV, ESV, GNB, GWN, ICB, ISV, JB,
[LB], MOF, MRC, MSG, NAB, NAS, NAU, NCV,
NEB, NET, NIrV, NIV, NJB, NLT, NRS, NWT, Phi,
REB, RSV, TCW, TNIV, WNT

୨ଡ଼   ୨ଡ଼   ୨ଡ଼

Acts 15:11 But we believe that through the
grace of the Lord Jesus ~~Christ~~ we shall be
saved, even as they.

Missing from: AMP, ASV, BBE, CEV, CJB, CSB,
DBY, ERV, ESV, GNB, GWN, HNV, ICB, JB, LB,
MOF, MRC, MSG, NAB, NAS, NAU, NCV, NEB,
NET, NIrV, NIV, NJB, NLT, NRS, NWT, Phi, REB,
RSV, TNIV, WEB, WNT

᪻   ᪻   ᪻

Acts 16:31 And they said, Believe on the Lord Jesus ~~Christ,~~ and thou shalt be saved, and thy house.

Missing from: *AMP*, ASV, BBE, CEV, CJB, CSB, DBY, DRA, ERV, ESV, GNB, GWN, HNV, ISV, LB, ICB, JB, LB, MOF, MRC, MSG, NAB, NAS, NAU, NCV, NEB, NET, NIrV, NIV, NJB, NLT, NRS, NWT, Phi, REB, RSV, TNIV, WNT

᪻   ᪻   ᪻

Acts 19:4 Then said Paul, John verily baptized with the baptism of repentance, saying unto the people, that they should believe on him which should come after him, that is, on ~~Christ~~ Jesus.

John didn't merely say that *Jesus* would come after him, but that Messiah —*Christ*— would come after him. And the Messiah was Jesus.

Missing from: [AMP], ASV, Bar, BBE, CEV, CJB, CSB, DBY, DRA, ERV, ESV, GNB, GWN, HNV, ICB, ISV, JB, LB, MOF, MRC, MSG, NAB, NAS, NAU, NCV, NEB, NET, NIrV, NIV, NJB, NLT, NRS, NWT, Phi, REB, RSV, TNIV, WEB, WNT

᪻   ᪻   ᪻

Acts 20:21 Testifying both to the Jews, and also to the Greeks, repentance toward God, and faith toward our Lord Jesus ~~Christ~~.

Missing from: ASV, Bar, CEV, CSB, GNB, GWN, HNV, ICB, ISV, JB, MSG, NCV, NAB, NCV, NEB, NET, NIrV, NIV, NJB, NLT, NRS, NWT, Phi, REB, TNIV, WEB, WNT

᪻   ᪻   ᪻

WHOSE GOSPEL ?!

Romans 1:16 For I am not ashamed of the gospel ~~of Christ~~: for it is the power of God unto salvation to every one that believeth; to the Jew first, and also to the Greek.

Isn't it strange that in the very verse where Paul says "I am not ashamed of the gospel," the Alexandrians removed whose gospel it is?

Missing from: AMP, ASV, Bar, BBE, CEV, CJB, CSB, DBY, DRA, ERV, ESV, GNB, GWN, ICB, ISV, JB, MOF, MRC, MSG, NAB, NAS, NAU, NCV, NEB, NET, NIrV, NIV, NJB, NRS, NWT, Phi, REB, RSV, TCW, TNIV, WNT

❦   ❦   ❦

Romans 16:20 And the God of peace shall bruise Satan under your feet shortly. The grace of our Lord Jesus ~~Christ~~ be with you. Amen.

Missing from: Bar, CEV, CJB, CSB, GNB, GWN, ICB, MRC, MSG[160] NAB, NAS, NAU, NCV, NEB, NET, NIrV, NIV, NLT, NWT, Phi, TNIV

❦   ❦   ❦

1 Corinthians 5:4 In the name of our Lord Jesus ~~Christ~~, when ye are gathered together, and my spirit, with the power of our Lord Jesus ~~Christ~~,

Missing from: AMP[161] ASV, Bar, BBE, CEV, CJB, DRA, ERV, ESV, GNB, GWN, ICB, ISV, JB, MOF[162] MRC, MSG, NAB, NAS, NAU, NCV,

---

160) The MSG says "Enjoy the best of Jesus," removing *both* "Christ" *and* "Lord."
161) The AMP and DRA delete only the second occurrence of "Christ." AMP italicizes the first.
162) Moffatt (MOF) keeps the first "Christ" but removes the second "Christ."

NEB, NET, NIrV, NIV, NJB, NLT, NRS, NWT, Phi, REB, RSV, TNIV, WNT

ℬ   ℬ   ℬ

(1 Corinthians 9:1) Am I not an apostle? am I not free? have I not seen Jesus ~~Christ~~ our Lord? are not ye my work in the Lord?

Missing from: AMP, ASV, Bar, BBE, CEV, CJB, CSB, DBY, ERV, ESV, GNB, GWN, ICB, ISV, JB, LB, MOF, MRC, MSG, NAB, NAS, NAU, NCV, NEB, NET, NIrV, NIV, NJB, NLT, NRS, NWT, Phi, REB, RSV, TNIV, WNT

ℬ   ℬ   ℬ

WHOSE GOSPEL?

(1 Corinthians 9:18) What is my reward then? Verily that, when I preach the gospel, I may make the gospel ~~of Christ~~ without charge, that I abuse not my power in the gospel.

As you will observe in the footnotes for this verse, not only did ancient Alexandrians remove "of Christ," but modern translators also removed words that God clearly repeated. Repetition is God's exclamation point. If God repeated words, what authority does a modern translator have to remove them?

Missing from: AMP, ASV, Bar, BBE, CEV, CJB[163], CSB, DBY, DRA, ERV, ESV, GNB, GWN, ICB, ISV, JB, LB, MOF, MRC, MSG[164], NAB, NAS, NAU, NCV, NEB, NET, NIrV, NIV, NJB, NLT, NRS, NWT, Phi, REB, RSV, TCW, TNIV, WNT

ℬ   ℬ   ℬ

THERE'S NO GOSPEL?

163) The CJB, MSG, NIV & WNT not only remove "of Christ," but also the 2nd and 3rd times Paul says "gospel," which is in *every* Greek manuscript.
164) The MSG also removes "that I abuse not my power in the gospel," which is in *every* Greek manuscript.

1 Corinthians 16:23 The grace of our Lord Jesus ~~Christ~~ be with you.

Missing from: *AMP*, Bar, CEV, CJB, CSB, ESV, GNB, GWN, ICB, ISV, JB, MOF, MRC, MSG, NAB, NAS, NAU, NCV, NET, NIrV, NIV, NLT, NRS, NWT, Phi, REB, RSV, TNIV, WNT

ഇ   ഇ   ഇ

2 Corinthians 11:31 The God and Father of ~~our~~ Lord Jesus ~~Christ~~, which is blessed for evermore, knoweth that I lie not.

Missing from: AMP[165] ASV, Bar, CEV[166] CJB, CSB, DBY, ERV, ESV, GNB, GWN, HNV, ISV, NAB, JB, MOF, MRC, MSG, NAS, NAU, NCV, NEB, NET, NIrV, NIV, NJB, NLT, NRS, NWT, Phi, REB, RSV, TNIV, WEB

ഇ   ഇ   ഇ

Galatians 3:17 And this I say, that the covenant, that was confirmed before of God ~~in Christ~~, the law, which was four hundred and thirty years after, cannot disannul, that it should make the promise of none effect.

The covenant was confirmed of God *in Christ*. Note how when Christ is removed, it reduces the influence of God's Son through history.

Missing from: [AMP], ASV, Bar, BBE, CEV, CJB, CSB, DBY, DRA, ERV, ESV, GNB, GWN, ICB, ISV, JB, LB, MOF, MRC, MSG, NAB, NAS, NAU, NCV, NEB, NET, NIrV, NIV, NJB, NLT, NRS, NWT, Phi, REB, RSV, TCW, TNIV, WNT

ഇ   ഇ   ഇ

---

165) The AMP, HNV, NCV and WEB keep "Christ" but remove "our." AMP italicizes "Christ."

166) The CEV, MSG and NLT keep "our" but remove "Christ."

[Handwritten margin notes: "NO CHRIST?" and "NO COVENANT!"]

HOW DO WE GET TO GOD?

Galatians 4:7 Wherefore thou art no more a servant, but a son; and if a son, then an heir of God through ~~Christ~~.

Here, "through Christ" is changed to "through God" in Alexandrian versions. But the *only* way to the Father is through the Son (Luke 10:22; 1 John 2:23). When Christ is removed from the verse, this truth is lost.

Missing from: *AMP*, ASV, Bar, BBE, CEV, CJB,CSB, DBY, DRA, ERV, ESV, GNB, GWN, ICB, ISV, JB, LB, MOF, MRC, MSG, NAB, NAS, NAU, NCV, NEB, NET, NIrV, NIV, NJB, NLT, NRS, NWT, Phi, REB, RSV, TNIV, WNT

ೀ ೀ ೀ

Philippians 4:13 I can do all things through ~~Christ~~ which strengtheneth me.

This is a powerful verse. But it loses its power when Christ is removed and it is no longer Christ that is strengthening us. Yet look at all the versions that remove this vital doctrine. That is why so many people with corrupted Bibles "accidentally" quote the King James when they come to this verse. *NIV CHANGES CHRIST TO "HIM"*

Missing from: ASV, Bar, BBE, CJB, CSB, DBY, DRA, ERV, ESV, ISV, JB, MOF, MRC, MSG, NAB, NAS, NAU, NEB, NET, NIV, NJB, NRS, NWT, Phi, REB, RSV, TNIV, WNT

ೀ ೀ ೀ

1 Thessalonians 2:19 For what is our hope, or joy, or crown of rejoicing? Are not even ye in the presence of our Lord Jesus ~~Christ~~ at his coming?

Missing from: AMP, ASV, Bar, BBE, CEV, CJB, CSB, DBY, ERV, ESV, GNB, GWN, HNV, ISV, JB, MOF,

MRC, MSG, NAB, NAS, NAU, NEB, NET, NIrV, NIV, NJB, NLT, NRS, NWT, Phi, REB, RSV, TNIV, WEB, WNT

❧   ❧   ❧

1 Thessalonians 3:11 Now God himself and our Father, and our Lord Jesus ~~Christ~~, direct our way unto you.

Missing from: *AMP*, Bar, CEV, GNB, ICB, ISV, LB, MOF, MRS, MSG, NAS, NAU, NCV, NEB, NIrV, NIV, NRS, NWT, Phi, REB, RSV, TNIV, WNT

❧   ❧   ❧

1 Thessalonians 3:13 To the end he may stablish your hearts unblameable in holiness before God, even our Father, at the coming of our Lord Jesus ~~Christ~~ with all his saints.

Missing from: *AMP*, ASV, Bar, BBE, CEV[167] CJB, CSB, DBY, ERV, ESV, GNB, GWN, HNV, ICB, ISV, MOF, MRC, MSG, NAB, NAS, NAU, NCV, NEB, NET, NIrV, NIV, NJB, NLT, NRS, NWT, Phi, REB, RSV, TCW, TNIV, WEB, WNT

❧   ❧   ❧

2 Thessalonians 1:8 In flaming fire taking vengeance on them that know not God, and that obey not the gospel of our Lord Jesus ~~Christ~~:

Missing from: *AMP*, ASV, Bar, BBE, CEV, CJB, CSB, ERV, ESV, GNB, GWN, HNV, ISV, JB, MOF, MRC, MSG[68] NAB, NAS, NAU, NEB, NET, NIrV, NIV, NJB, NLT, NRS, NWT, Phi, REB, RSV, TNIV, WEB, WNT

❧   ❧   ❧

---

167) The CEV not only removes "Christ," but also "Jesus."
168) The MSG not only removes "Christ;" it also takes away "of our Lord Jesus."

WHO IS THE LORD?

2 Thessalonians 1:12 That the name of our Lord Jesus ~~Christ~~ may be glorified in you, and ye in him, according to the grace of our God and the Lord Jesus Christ.

Missing from: *AMP*, ASV, Bar, BBE, CEV, CJB, CSB, *DBY*, DRA, ERV, ESV, GNB, GWN, HNV, ISV, MOF, MSG⁶⁹, NAB, NAS, NAU, NEB, NET, NIrV, NIV, NLT, NRS, NWT, Phi, REB, RSV, TNIV, WEB, WNT

૭ ૭ ૭

1 Timothy 2:7 Whereunto I am ordained a preacher, and an apostle, (I speak the truth ~~in Christ~~, and lie not;) a teacher of the Gentiles in faith and verity.

Missing from: ASV, Bar, BBE, CEV, CJB, CSB, DBY, DRA, ERV, ESV, GNB, GWN, ICB, ISV, JB, LB, MOF, MRC, MSG, NAB, NAS, NAU, NCV, NEB, NET, NIrV, NIV, NJB, NLT, NRS, NWT, Phi, REB, RSV, TCW, TNIV, WNT

૭ ૭ ૭

Hebrews 3:1 Wherefore, holy brethren, partakers of the heavenly calling, consider the Apostle and High Priest of our profession, ~~Christ~~ Jesus;

How amazing: this Apostle and High Priest is also the Messiah. But all the versions below remove this vital truth from this verse.

Missing from: AMP, ASV, Bar, BBE, CEV, CJB, CSB, DBY, DRA, ERV, ESV, GNB, GWN, HNV, ICB, ISV, JB, LB, MOF, MRC, MSG, NAB, NAS, NAU,

---

169) The MSG removes both "Christ" and "Lord."

NCV, NEB[170], NET, NIrV[171], NIV, NJB, NLT, NRS, NWT, REB, RSV, TCW[172], TNIV, WEB, WNT

∽   ∽   ∽

1 John 1:7 But if we walk in the light, as he is in the light, we have fellowship one with another, and the blood of Jesus ~~Christ~~ his Son cleanseth us from all sin.

Missing from: *AMP*, ASV, Bar, BBE, CEV, CJB, CSB, ERV, ESV, GNB, GWN, ICB, ISV, JB, LB, MOF, MRC, MSG, NAB, NAS, NAU, NCV, NEB, NET, NIrV, NIV, NJB, NLT, NRS, NWT, Phi, RSV, TNIV, WNT

∽   ∽   ∽

1 John 4:3 And every spirit that confesseth not ~~that~~ Jesus ~~Christ is come in the flesh~~ is not of God: and this is that spirit of antichrist, whereof ye have heard that it should come; and even now already is it in the world.

It is not just denying "Jesus," but that "Jesus Christ hath come in the flesh." Many Jewish people believe that Jesus existed, but not that the Messiah has already come, much less that the Messiah was—and is—Jesus.

Missing from: *AMP*, ASV, Bar, BBE, CEV, CJB, CSB, DRA, ERV, ESV, GNB, ICB, ISV, JB, LB, MOF[173], MRC, MSG, NAB, NAS, NAU, NCV, NEB, NET, NIrV, NIV, NJB, NLT, NRS, NWT, Phi, REB, RSV, TCW, TNIV, WNT

∽   ∽   ∽

---

170) The NEB took out "Christ," and also "Jesus," which is in *every* manuscript.
171) The NIrV put back in "Jesus" to make the sentence easy to understand, but still removed "Christ."
172) TCW has "Christ's" but is missing "Jesus."
173) Moffatt (MOF) removed "Christ" but summarized "is come in the flesh" by saying "incarnate."

(handwritten margin note: IS JESUS THE CHRIST?!)

Revelation 1:9 I John, who also am your brother, and companion in tribulation, and in the kingdom and patience of Jesus ~~Christ~~, was in the isle that is called Patmos, for the word of God, and for the testimony of Jesus ~~Christ~~.

Missing from: *AMP*, ASV, Bar, BBE, CEV, CJB, CSB, DBY, DRA[174], ERV, ESV, GNB, GWN, ICB, ISV, JB, LB, MOF, MRC, MSG, NAB, NAS, NAU, NCV[175], NEB, NET, NIrV, NIV, NJB, NLT, NRS, NWT, Phi, REB, RSV, TNIV, WNT

Revelation 12:17 And the dragon was ~~wroth with the woman~~, and went to make war with the remnant of her seed, which keep the commandments of God, and have the testimony of Jesus ~~Christ~~.

Missing from: *AMP*, ASV, Bar, BBE, CEV, CJB, CSB, DBY, ERV, ESV, GNB, GWN, HNV, ICB, ISV, JB, LB, MOF, MRC, MSG, NAB, NAS, NAU, NCV, NEB, NET, NIrV, NIV, NJB, NLT, NRS, NWT, Phi, REB, RSV, TCW, TNIV, WEB, WNT

Revelation 22:21 The grace of our Lord Jesus ~~Christ~~ be with you all. Amen.

The last verse of the Bible ends with the full nature of God's Son clearly displayed: "our Lord Jesus Christ," except in all the versions below, that is.

Missing from: *AMP*, ASV, Bar, BBE, CEV, CJB, CSB,

---

174) The DRA is only missing the first occurrence of "Christ."
175) The NCV keeps the first "Christ" and removes the first "Jesus," which is in every manuscript, though it removes the second "Christ."

ERV, ESV, GNB, GWN, ICB, ISV, JB, MOF, MRC, MSG, NAB, NAS, NAU, NCV, NEB, NET, NIrV, NIV, NJB, NLT, NRS, Phi, REB, RSV, TNIV, WNT

WHAT'S MISSING?
"JESUS CHRIST" OR "CHRIST JESUS" *P. 168-169*

(handwritten in left margin: IS JESUS CHRIST LORD?)

(1 Corinthians 16:22) If any man love not the Lord ~~Jesus Christ~~, let him be Anathema Maranatha.

Missing from: AMP, ASV, Bar, BBE, CEV, CJB, CSB, *DBY*, ERV, ESV, GNB, GWN, ICB, ISV, JB, LB, MOF, MRC, MSG, NAB, NAS, NAU, NCV, NEB, NET, NIrV, NIV, NJB, NLT, NRS, NWT, Phi, REB, RSV, TCW, TNIV, WNT

❧   ❧   ❧

Galatians 6:15 ~~For in Christ Jesus~~ neither circumcision availeth any thing, nor uncircumcision, but a new creature.

Paul is not saying circumcision doesn't matter to the Jewish people; He is saying that circumcision does nothing special for a *Christian.*

Missing from: ASV, Bar, BBE, CEV, CJB, CSB, *DBY*, ERV, ESV, GNB, GWN, ICB, ISV, JB, LB, MOF, MRC, MSG, NAB, NAS, NAU, NCV, NEB, NET, NIrV, NIV, NJB, NLT, NRS, NWT, REB, RSV, TNIV, WNT

❧   ❧   ❧

Ephesians 3:9 And to make all men see what is the fellowship of the mystery, which from the beginning of the world hath been hid in God, who created all things ~~by Jesus Christ~~:

There is a world of difference between God creating all

things (every monotheist[176] believes that) and God creating all things *by Jesus Christ.* Removing "by Jesus Christ" takes away the Lord Jesus Christ's role as Creator.

Missing from: *AMP*, ASV, Bar, BBE, CEV, CJB, CSB, DBY, DRA, ERV, ESV, GNB, GWN, ICB, ISV, JB, LB, MOF, MRC, MSG, NAB, NAS, NAU, NCV, NEB, NET, NIrV, NIV, NJB, NLT, NRS, NWT, Phi, REB, RSV, TCW, TNIV, WNT

❧ ❧ ❧

2 Timothy 4:22 The Lord ~~Jesus Christ~~ be with thy spirit. Grace be with you. Amen.

Missing from: *AMP*, ASV, Bar, BBE, CEV, CJB, CSB, ERV, ESV, GNB, GWN, ICB, ISV, JB, MOF, MRC, MSG[177], NAB, NAS, NAU, NCV, NEB, NET, NIrV, NIV, NJB, NLT, NRS, NWT, Phi, REB, RSV, TNIV, WNT

WHAT'S MISSING? "LORD JESUS CHRIST" P. 169-170

Romans 16:24 ~~The grace of our Lord Jesus Christ be with you all. Amen.~~

Missing from: *AMP*, *ASV*, Bar, BBE, CEV, CJB, [CSB], ERV, ESV, GNB, GWN, ICB, *ISV*, JB, MOF, *MRC*, MSG, NAB, [NAS], [NAU], NCV, NEB, NET, NIrV, NIV, NLT, NRS, NWT, Phi, REB, RSV, TNIV, WNT

❧ ❧ ❧

Ephesians 3:14 For this cause I bow my knees unto the Father ~~of our Lord Jesus Christ,~~

Missing from: *AMP*, ASV, Bar, BBE, CEV, CJB, CSB, *DBY*, ERV, ESV, GNB ,GWN, ICB, JB, LB, MOF, MRC, MSG, NAB, NAS, NAU, NCV, NEB,

---

176) A *monotheist* is anyone who believes there is only one God. Many non-Christian religions are monotheistic.
177) The MSG eliminates "the Lord Jesus Christ" and substitutes "God."

NET, NIrV, NIV, NLT, NRS, NWT, Phi, REB, RSV, TCW, TNIV, WNT

❧   ❧   ❧

Colossians 1:2 To the saints and faithful brethren in Christ which are at Colosse: Grace be unto you, and peace, from God our Father ~~and the Lord Jesus Christ~~.

The Alexandrians took away the greeting from the Lord Jesus Christ. Would you want someone to remove your name from a greeting?

Missing from: AMP, ASV, Bar, BBE, CEV, CJB, CSB, *DBY*, ERV, ESV, GNB, GWN, ICB, ISV, JB, LB, MOF, MRC, MSG, NAB, NAS, NAU, NCV, NEB, NET, NIrV, NIV, NJB, NLT, NRS, NWT, Phi, REB, RSV, TNIV, WNT

MISSING WORDS CONCERNING THE GODHEAD

P. 171

I was told in Bible college and seminary "it doesn't matter" that all these words and phrases weren't in the Alexandrian Bibles. All that mattered was that there were "enough scriptures where you can find the doctrines."

But that is the problem. It's not just a few words. Time and time again Alexandrians removed words that clarify who and what God the Father, Son and Holy Ghost are.

Is it any wonder that people are starting to question the deity of Jesus Christ (or that He is the only way to heaven) in evangelical churches and societies? It started with tainted Bibles, and it led to their tainted faith.

WHAT'S MISSING?
THE GODHEAD (FATHER, SON AND HOLY GHOST)

> 1 John 5:7 For there are three that bear re-
> cord ~~in heaven, the Father, the Word, and the~~
> ~~Holy Ghost: and these three are one~~.

This is one of the clearest statements of the Godhead: the Father, Son and Holy Ghost being one God. It was removed early on by institutional "churches" that argued over the Godhead. For them it was far easier to take away God's words than admit they were wrong.

But enough copies of God's words were preserved that kept this important doctrine alive all the way through the Dark Ages, and available to you through the King James Bible.

Missing from: *AMP*, ASV, Bar, BBE, CEV, CJB, CSB, DBY, ERV, ESV, GNB, GWN, HNV, ICB, ISV, JB, LB, MOF, MRC, MSG, NAB, NAS, NAU, NCV, NEB, NET, NIrV, NIV, NJB, NLT, NRS, NWT, Phi, REB, RSV, TNIV, WEB, WNT

෧ ෧ ෧

> 1 John 5:8 ~~And there are three that bear wit-~~
> ~~ness in earth~~, the Spirit, and the water, and
> the blood: and these three agree in one.

Missing from: ASV, Bar, BBE, CEV, CJB, CSB, DBY, ERV, ESV, GNB, GWN, HNV, ICB, ISV, JB, LB, MOF, MRC, MSG, NAB, NAS, NAU, NCV, NEB, NET, NIrV[178], NIV, NJB, NLT, NRS, NWT, Phi, REB, RSV, TNIV, WEB, WNT

---

178) Not only does the NIrV remove the crucial doctrine of the Godhead, it also changes the "Spirit, and the water, and the blood" into "the Holy Spirit, the baptism of Jesus and his death."

WHAT'S MISSING? "GOD"

Matthew 6:33 But seek ye first the kingdom of God, and his righteousness; and all these things shall be added unto you.

Missing from: AMP, ASV, BBE, CJB, ERV, GWN, JB, LB, MRC, NAS, NAU, NET, NIV, NJB, NRS, NWT, Phi, RSV, TNIV, WNT

✥   ✥   ✥

Matthew 19:17 And he said unto him, Why callest thou me good? *there is* none good but one, *that is,* God: but if thou wilt enter into life, keep the commandments.

This verse makes it clear there is no human who is good. The only One who is good is God. So if Jesus is truly good, who does that make Him?

Missing from: ASV, Bar, BBE, CJB, CSB, DBY, ERV, ESV, GNB, GWN, ISV, JB, MRC, MOF, NAB, NAS, NAU, NEB, NET, NIV, NIrV, NLT, NRS, NWT, Phi, REB, RSV, TNIV, WNT

✥   ✥   ✥

Luke 4:4 And Jesus answered him, saying, It is written, That man shall not live by bread alone, but by every word of God.

The vital part of this verse, that we live "by every word of God" is missing in all the following versions. Even non-Christians can quote this verse (and do) when you remove the "offensive" second part of the sentence.

Missing from: *AMP*, ASV, Bar, BBE, CEV, CJB, CSB, ERV, ESV, GNB, GWN, ICB, JB, LB, MOF, MRC, MSG, NAB, NAS, NAU, NCV, NEB, NET, NIrV, NIV, NJB, NLT, NRS, NWT, Phi, REB, RSV, TNIV, WNT

❧   ❧   ❧

Luke 21:4 For all these have of their abundance cast *in* unto the offerings ~~of God~~[179] but she of her penury hath cast in all the living that she had.

Missing from: AMP, ASV, Bar, BBE, CEV, CJB, CSB, *DBY*, ERV, ESV, GNB, GWN, ICB, ISV, JB, LB, MOF, MRC, MSG, NAB, NAS, NAU, NCV, NEB, NET, NIrV, NIV, NJB, NLT, NRS, NWT, Phi, REB, RSV, TCW, TNIV, WNT

❧   ❧   ❧

Acts 20:25 And now, behold, I know that ye all, among whom I have gone preaching the kingdom ~~of God~~, shall see my face no more.

Missing from: AMP, ASV, Bar, BBE, CJB, CSB, *DBY*, ERV, ESV, *GWN*, JB, LB, MOF, MRC, NAB, NAS, NAU, NEB, NET, NIrV, NIV, NJB, NLT, NRS, NWT, REB, RSV, TCW[180], TNIV, WNT

❧   ❧   ❧

Acts 23:9 And there arose a great cry: and the scribes *that were* of the Pharisees' part arose, and strove, saying, We find no evil in this man: but if a spirit or an angel hath spoken to him, ~~let us not fight against God~~.

The most potent part of the verse has been removed. We can make a mistake about "a spirit" speaking to a man. But it is vitally important not to "fight against God."

---

179) Some versions go so far as to remove the whole concept of "casting in unto the offerings of God" and hide the missing words by saying "gave" or "contributed" instead.

180) TCW removes "kingdom of God" and substitutes "gospel," which appears in *no* Greek texts anywhere.

Missing from: *AMP*, ASV, Bar, BBE, CEV, CJB, CSB, DBY, DRA, ERV, ESV, GNB, GWN, ICB, ISV, JB, LB, MOF, MRC, NAB, NAS, NAU, NCV, NEB, NET, NIrV, NIV, NJB, NLT, NRS, NWT, Phi, REB, RSV, TNIV, WNT

ക്ക   ക്ക   ക്ക

1 Timothy 3:16 And without controversy great is the mystery of godliness: ~~God~~ was manifest in the flesh, justified in the Spirit, seen of angels, preached unto the Gentiles, believed on in the world, received up into glory.

How much more plain can a scripture be? "GOD" was in the flesh. But Alexandrians sneakily changed the word "God" to "who" by removing a single line from a Greek letter. That changed "God" to a mere "who" or "which." They deleted Christ's godhood by removing a single line.

Missing from: [AMP], ASV, Bar, BBE, CEV[181], CJB, CSB, DRA, ERV, ESV, GNB, GWN, ICB, ISV, JB, LB[182], MOF, MRC, MSG, NAB, NAS, NAU, NCV, NEB, NET, NIrV[183], NIV, NJB, NLT, NRS, NWT, Phi, REB, RSV, TNIV, WNT

ക്ക   ക്ക   ക്ക

1 John 5:13 These things have I written unto you that believe on the name of the Son of God; that ye may know that ye have eternal life, ~~and that ye may believe on the name of the Son of God.~~

---

181) The CEV, NLT & WNT hide the missing word "God" by substituting "Christ."
182) The LB substitutes "Jesus." See note for the NIrV following.
183) The NIrV hides its missing words "God was manifest in the flesh" by substituting "Jesus appeared in a body." That's obvious. *All* humans "appear in a body." The point is that unlike anyone else in the history of earth, *God Himself* became flesh and bone. No "alternate translation" can make up for that fatal omission.

Missing from: AMP, ASV, Bar, BBE, CEV, CJB, CSB, DBY, DRA, ERV, ESV, GNB, GWN, ICB, ISV, JB, LB, MOF, MRC, MSG, NAB, NAS, NAU, NCV, NEB, NET, NIrV, NIV, NJB, NLT, NRS, NWT, Phi, REB, RSV, TNIV, WNT

๛   ๛   ๛

(Revelation 14:5) And in their mouth was found no guile: for they are without fault ~~before the throne of God~~.

Missing from: *AMP*, ASV, Bar, BBE, CEV, CJB, CSB, DBY, ERV, ESV, GNB, GWN, HNV, ICB, ISV, JB, LB, MOF, MRC, MSG, NAB, NAS, NAU, NCV, NEB, NET, NIrV, NIV, NJB, NLT, NRS, NWT, Phi, REB, RSV, TNIV, WEB, WNT

๛   ๛   ๛

Revelation 20:9 And they went up on the breadth of the earth, and compassed the camp of the saints about, and the beloved city: and fire came down from ~~God out of~~ heaven, and devoured them.

Missing from: AMP, ASV, Bar, BBE, CEV, CJB, CSB, *DBY*, ERV, ESV, GNB, GWN, ICB, JB, MOF, MRC, MSG, NAB, NAS, NAU, NCV, NEB, NET, NIrV, NIV, NJB, NLT, NRS, NWT, Phi, REB, RSV, TNIV, WNT

WHAT'S MISSING? T. 175–177
THE FATHER (OF THE LORD JESUS CHRIST)

Which "Father" is this? Read the next verse very carefully. New Agers and Luciferians use the prayer in Luke to refer to Lucifer, "the angel of light" or of wisdom. But that is only possible if you eliminate the words that distinguish the true God from the fallen angel.

Read Luke 11:2-4, and you will see why *all* of these words belong in your Bible.

> Luke 11:2 And he said unto them, When ye pray, say, ~~Our~~ Father ~~which art in heaven~~, Hallowed be thy name. Thy kingdom come. ~~Thy will be done, as in heaven, so in earth~~.

Note that all those words distinguish the God of heaven from an angel fallen from heaven.

> Missing from: *AMP*, ASV, Bar, BBE, CEV, CJB, CSB, DBY, DRA, ERV, ESV, GNB, GWN, ICB, ISV, JB, LB, MOF, MRC, MSG, NAB, NAS, NAU, NCV, NEB, NET, NIrV, NIV, NJB, NLT, NRS, NWT, Phi, REB, RSV, TCW[184], TNIV, WNT

❧ ❧ ❧

> Luke 11:4 And forgive us our sins; for we also forgive every one that is indebted to us. And lead us not into temptation; ~~but deliver us from evil~~.

These words distinguish God the Father from the Devil. Only the Father delivers us from evil.

> Missing from: *AMP*, ASV, Bar, BBE, CEV, CJB, CSB, DBY, DRA, ERV, ESV, GNB, GWN, ICB, ISV, JB, LB, MOF, MRC, NAB, NAS, NAU, NCV, NEB, NET, NIrV, NIV, NJB, NLT, NRS, NWT, Phi, REB, RSV, TNIV, WNT

❧ ❧ ❧

> John 16:10 Of righteousness, because I go to ~~my~~ Father, and ye see me no more;

Changing "my" to "the" seems like such a *little* change. But Alexandrians put "the" instead of "my" because 1) it

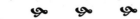

---

184) TCW is only missing *one* of all these words: "Our."

takes away from Jesus' deity, that God is not just "the" Father, but "my" (Jesus') *literal* Father, and 2) then they could remove what Jesus said six verses later (see verse 16). The Devil was quite sneaky removing verses that teach the Godhood of Christ.

> Missing from: ASV, BBE, CEV, CJB, CSB, *DBY*, DRA, ERV, ESV, GNB, GWN, ICB, ISV, JB, LB, MOF, MRC, MSG, NAB, NAS, NAU, NCV, NEB, NET, NIrV, NIV, NJB, NLT, NRS, NWT, Phi, REB, RSV, TCW, TNIV, WNT

ও   ও   ও

> (John 16:16) A little while, and ye shall not see me: and again, a little while, and ye shall see me, ~~because I go to the Father~~.

It is amazing that these words are missing. The disciples quote back Jesus' words in the very next verse. It doesn't make sense for them to "repeat" something Jesus never said.

> Missing from: AMP, ASV, Bar, BBE, CEV, CJB, CSB, *DBY*, ERV, ESV, GNB, GWN, HNV, ISV, JB, LB, MOF, MRC, MSG, NAB, NAS, NAU, NCV, NEB, NET, NIrV, NIV, NJB, NLT, NRS, NWT, Phi, REB, RSV, TNIV, WEB, WNT

WHAT'S MISSING? ONLY "BEGOTTEN" SON P. 177-186

> (John 1:14) And the Word was made flesh, and dwelt among us, (and we beheld his glory, the glory as of the only ~~begotten~~ of the Father,) full of grace and truth.

This has nothing to do with the Greek manuscripts. This has to do with English translation. The Greek word "monogenees" was translated "only begotten" throughout history —until the 20th century. Modern "scholars" chose to change the English to hide the true meaning, "only begotten."

Why would they do that? Jesus is the only *begotten* Son. All Christians are *adopted* sons [185], but not "begotten." Taking out the English word "begotten" wrongly makes God into a liar.

Missing from: Bar, BBE, CEV, CJB, CSB, ESV, GNB, GWN, HNV, ICB, ISV, JB, LB, MOF, MSG, NAB, NCV, NEB, NET, NIrV, NIV, NJB, NLT, NRS, Phi, REB, RSV, TCW [186], TNIV [187], WEB, WNT

ళ   ళ   ళ

John 1:18 No man hath seen God at any time; the only ~~begotten~~ [188] Son, which is in the bosom of the Father, he hath declared him.

Missing from: Bar, BBE, CEV, CJB, CSB, ESV, GNB, GWN, ICB, ISV, JB, LB, MOF, MSG, NAB [189], NCV, NEB, NET, NIrV, NIV, NJB, NRS, Phi, REB, RSV, TCW [190], TNIV, WEB, WNT

ళ   ళ   ళ

John 1:18 No man hath seen God at any time; the only begotten ~~Son~~, which is in the bosom of the Father, he hath declared *him*.

Here, "Son" is changed to "God." Some versions even

---

185) Romans 8:15; Galatians 4:5; Ephesians 1:5.
186) TCW removes "only begotten of the Father" and adds "from God," found in *no* manuscript, anywhere.
187) The TNIV's solution is to call Jesus "the one and only," with "Son" in half-brackets.
188) See the previous note.
189) The NAB also adds "God."
190) TCW not only removes "begotten," it even removes "only," taking away a Greek word (only-begotten) that is in *every* Greek manuscript. What is TCW saying about Jesus?

call Jesus a *begotten* God. He is not *a* God —He is *the* God, known as God the Son.

Missing from: AMP[191], ESV[192], MRC, MSG, NAS, NAU, NET[193], NIV[194], NLT, NWT

John 3:16 For God so loved the world, that he gave his only ~~begotten~~ Son, that whosoever believeth in him should not perish, but have everlasting life.

Missing from: Bar, BBE, CEV, CJB, CSB, ESV, GNB, GWN, HNV, ICB, ISV, JB, LB, MOF, MSG, NAB, NCV, NEB, NET, NIrV, NIV, NJB, NLT, NRS, Phi, REB, RSV, TCW, TNIV, WEB, WNT

John 3:18 He that believeth on him is not condemned: but he that believeth not is condemned already, because he hath not believed in the name of the only ~~begotten~~ Son of God.

Missing from: Bar, BBE, CEV, CJB, CSB, ESV, GNB, GWN, HNV, ICB, ISV, JB, LB, MOF, MSG, NAB, NCV, NEB, NET, NIrV, NIV, NJB, NLT, NRS, Phi, REB, RSV, TCW[195], TNIV, WEB, WNT

---

191) The Amplified Bible (AMP) adds "the only begotten God" as one of the optional readings.
192) The ESV says "the only God," adding "God" and removing "begotten."
193) The NET says "The only one, himself God," adding "one," "himself" and "God," and removing "begotten."
194) The current version of the NIV reads "God the One and Only," which sounds nice, but it is still *not* what the Greek text says.
195) TCW not only removes "begotten," it even removes "only," taking a way a Greek word (only-begotten) that is in *every* Greek manuscript. What is TCW saying about Jesus?

1 John 4:9 In this was manifested the love of God toward us, because that God sent his only ~~begotten~~ Son into the world, that we might live through him.

Missing from: Bar, BBE, CEV, CJB, CSB, ESV, GNB, GWN, HNV, ICB, ISV, JB, LB, MOF, MSG, NAB, NCV, NEB, NET, NIV, NJB, NLT, NRS, Phi, REB, RSV, TCW, TNIV, WEB, WNT

WHAT'S MISSING: MARY'S "FIRSTBORN" SON

Matthew 1:25 And knew her not till she had brought forth ~~her firstborn~~ son: and he called his name JESUS.

This is no small change. Take away those two words and you can change Mary from a woman who was blessed with children (James, Joses, Simon, Judas, as well as daughters), into the ever-virgin Mary goddess of Roman Catholicism.

Missing from: *AMP*, ASV, Bar, BBE, CEV, CJB, CSB, ERV, ESV, GNB, GWN, ICB, ISV, JB, LB, MRC, MSG, MOF, NAB, NAS, NAU, NCV, NEB, NET, NIrV, NIV, NJB, NLT, NRS, NWT, Phi, REB, RSV, TCW, TNIV, WNT

WHAT'S MISSING: THE SON OF GOD

Mark 1:1 The beginning of the gospel of Jesus Christ, ~~the Son of God;~~

Missing from: *AMP*, MSG, NWT, TNIV

What's Missing: The Eternal Son

Revelation 1:8 I am Alpha and Omega, ~~the beginning and the ending~~, saith the Lord, which is, and which was, and which is to come, the Almighty.

Missing from: *AMP*, ASV, BBE, CEV, CJB, CSB, DBY, ERV, ESV, GNB[196], GWN, HNV, ICB, ISV, JB, MOF, MRC, MSG, NAB, NAS, NAU, NCV, NET, NIV, NEB, NJB, NRS, NWT, Phi, REB, RSV, TCW, TNIV, WEB, WNT

❧   ❧   ❧

Revelation 1:11 Saying, ~~I am Alpha and Omega, the first and the last: and~~, What thou seest, write in a book, and send it unto the seven churches which are in Asia; unto Ephesus, and unto Smyrna, and unto Pergamos, and unto Thyatira, and unto Sardis, and unto Philadelphia, and unto Laodicea.

Missing from: *AMP*, ASV, Bar, BBE, CEV, CJB, CSB, DBY, DRA, ERV, ESV, GNB, GWN, HNV, ICB, ISV, JB, MOF, MRC, MSG, NAB, NAS, NAU, NCV, NEB, NET, NIrV, NIV, NJB, NLT, NRS, NWT, Phi, REB, RSV, TCW, TNIV, WEB, WNT

❧   ❧   ❧

Revelation 5:14 And the four beasts said, Amen. And the four *and* twenty elders fell down and worshipped ~~him that liveth for ever and ever~~.

Missing from: *AMP*, ASV, Bar, BBE, CEV, CJB, CSB, DBY, ERV, ESV, GNB, GWN, HNV, ICB, ISV, JB,

---

196) The GNB does the opposite: it has "I am the first and the last," but is missing "Alpha and Omega."

LB, MOF, MRC, MSG, NAB, NAS, NAU, NCV,
NEB, NET, NIrV, NIV, NJB, NLT[197], NRS, NWT,
Phi, REB, RSV, TNIV, WEB, WNT

Revelation 11:17 Saying, We give thee thanks,
O Lord God Almighty, which art, and wast,
~~and art to come~~; because thou hast taken to
thee thy great power, and hast reigned.

When you remove "and art to come," you take away
the eternal nature of the Lord Jesus Christ.

> Missing from: AMP, ASV, Bar, BBE, CEV, CJB, CSB,
> DBY, ERV, ESV, GNB, GWN, HNV, ICB, ISV, JB,
> LB, MOF, MRC, MSG, NAB, NAS, NAU, NCV,
> NEB, NET, NIrV, NIV, NJB, NLT, NRS, NWT, Phi,
> REB, RSV, TNIV, WEB, WNT

WHAT'S MISSING? ONLY "GOD" IS "GOOD"

> Matthew 19:16 And, behold, one came and
> said unto him, ~~Good~~ Master, what good
> thing shall I do, that I may have eternal life?

The man forgot that only "God" is "good." Maybe the
man called Jesus "good" to flatter Him, but Jesus set him
straight in the next verse. Remember: the man had no idea
that God was actually standing right in front of him.

> Missing from: AMP, ASV, Bar, BBE, CEV, CJB, CSB,
> DBY, ERV, ESV, GNB, GWN, ICB, ISV, JB, MRC,
> MOF, MSG, NAB, NAS, NAU, NCV, NEB, NET,
> NIrV, NIV, NJB, NLT, NRS, NWT, Phi, REB, RSV,
> TCW, TNIV, WNT

---

197) The NLT not only removes "him that liveth for ever and ever," but also *adds*
"the Lamb" in its place.

❧   ❧   ❧

Matthew 19:17 And he said unto him, Why callest thou me good? *there is* none good but one, *that is*, ~~God~~: but if thou wilt enter into life, keep the commandments.

Many things are wrong with this verse. After Alexandrians removed "Good" from "Good master" in verse 16, then changed verse 17 to read something like "Why do you ask me about what is good?" – which is nothing like what Jesus really said: "Why callest thou me good?" All those Bibles remove the teaching about Who is truly "good." *Only God* is good.

Missing from: ASV, Bar, BBE, CJB, CSB, DBY, ERV, ESV, GNB, GWN, ISV, JB, MRC, MOF, NAB, NAS, NAU, NEB, NET, NIV, NIrV, NLT, NRS, NWT, Phi, REB, RSV, TNIV, WNT

WHAT'S MISSING?
THE HOLY SPIRIT AND MAN'S SPIRIT

Romans 8:1 *There is* therefore now no condemnation to them which are in Christ Jesus, ~~who walk not after the flesh, but after the Spirit~~.

Missing from: *AMP*, ASV, Bar, BBE, CEV, CJB, CSB, DBY, ERV, ESV, GNB, GWN, ICB, ISV, JB, LB, MOF, MRC, MSG, NAB, NAS, NAU, NCV, NEB, NET, NIrV, NIV, NJB, NLT, NRS, NWT, Phi, REB, RSV, TCW, TNIV, WNT

❧   ❧   ❧

1 Peter 1:22 Seeing ye have purified your souls in obeying the truth ~~through the Spirit~~

unto unfeigned love of the brethren, *see that ye* love one another with a pure heart fervently:

Missing from: *AMP*, ASV, Bar, BBE, CEV, CJB, CSB, DBY, DRA, ERV, ESV, GNB, GWN, ICB, ISV, JB, LB, MOF, NAB, MRC, MSG, NAS, NAU, NCV, NEB, NET, NIrV, NIV, NJB, NLT, NRS, NWT, Phi, REB, RSV, TNIV, WNT

ക്ക   ക്ക   ക്ക

Luke 2:40 And the child grew, and waxed strong ~~in spirit~~, filled with wisdom: and the grace of God was upon him.

Missing from: *AMP*, ASV, Bar, BBE, CEV, CJB, CSB, *DBY*, DRA, ERV, ESV, GNB, GWN, ICB, ISV, JB, LB, MOF, MRC, NAB, NAU, NCV, NEB, NET, NIrV, NIV, NJB, NLT, NRS, NWT, Phi, REB, RSV, TNIV, WNT

ക്ക   ക്ക   ക്ക

1 Corinthians 6:20 For ye are bought with a price: therefore glorify God in your body, ~~and in your spirit, which are God's.~~

Missing from: AMP, ASV, Bar, BBE, CEV, CJB, CSB, DBY, DRA, ERV, ESV, GNB, GWN, ICB, ISV, JB, LB, MOF, MRC, MSG, NAB, NAS, NAU, NCV, NEB, NET, NIrV, NIV, NJB, NLT, NRS, NWT, Phi, REB, RSV, TCW, TNIV, WNT

ക്ക   ക്ക   ക്ക

1 Timothy 4:12 Let no man despise thy youth; but be thou an example of the believers, in word, in conversation, in charity, ~~in spirit~~, in faith, in purity.

Missing from: AMP, ASV, Bar, BBE, CEV, CSB, DBY, DRA, ERV, ESV, GNB, GWN, ICB, ISV, JB,

LB, MOF, MRC, MSG, NAB, NAS, NAU, NCV, NEB, NET, NIrV, NIV, NJB, NLT, NRS, NWT, Phi, REB, RSV, TCW, TNIV, WNT

MISSING WORDS CONCERNING THE GOSPEL MESSAGE

WHAT'S MISSING?
BELIEF IN CHRIST FOR SALVATION

John 6:47 Verily, verily, I say unto you, He that believeth ~~on me~~ hath everlasting life.

People in New Age cults like Religious Science and Unity love the Alexandrian perversion of this verse. It just says to "believe." But we must believe *on the Lord Jesus Christ* to be saved. [198]

Missing from: *AMP*, ASV, Bar, CJB, CSB, *DBY*, ERV, ESV, GNB, GWN, ICB, JB, MOF, MRC, NAB, NAS, NAU, NCV, NEB, NET, NIrV, NIV, NJB, NLT, NRS, NWT, Phi[199], REB, RSV, TNIV, WNT

Acts 8:37 ~~And Philip said, If thou believest with all thine heart, thou mayest. And he answered and said, I believe that Jesus Christ is the Son of God.~~

This is a major salvation verse, saying we must believe in Jesus with all our heart before we can be baptized. This is the *only* verse that tells what must happen before one can be baptized. (See Chapter 2.)

198) See John 14:6; Acts 4:12 and 16:31.
199) JB Phillips (Phi) strangely changed "on me" to "on him," meaning *the Father*, not *the Lord Jesus Christ*.

Missing from: *AMP*, *ASV*, Bar, BBE, CEV, CJB, [CSB], DBY, ERV, ESV, GNB, GWN, HNV, ICB, *ISV*, JB, MOF, *MRC*, MSG, NAB, [NAS], [NAU], NCV, NEB, NET, NIrV, NIV, NJB, NLT, NRS, NWT, Phi, REB, RSV, TNIV, WNT

WHAT'S MISSING?
CHRIST DIED "FOR US"

1 Corinthians 5:7 Purge out therefore the old leaven, that ye may be a new lump, as ye are unleavened. For even Christ our passover is sacrificed ~~for us~~:

Christ was sacrificed, not for His own sake, but for ours.

Missing from: AMP, ASV, BBE, CEV, CJB, CSB, DBY, DRA, ERV, ESV, GNB, GWN, ISV, JB, MOF, MRC, MSG, NAB, NAS, NAU, NCV, NEB, NET, NIV, NJB, NRS, NWT, REB, RSV, TNIV

൵   ൵   ൵

1 Peter 4:1 Forasmuch then as Christ hath suffered ~~for us~~ in the flesh, arm yourselves likewise with the same mind: for he that hath suffered in the flesh hath ceased from sin;

Again, Christ's suffering was not for Himself. It was not in vain. He suffered, bled and died *for us*, so we could live with Him.

Missing from: *AMP*, ASV, Bar, BBE, CEV, CJB, CSB, DRA, ERV, ESV, GNB, GWN, ICB, ISV, JB, LB, MRC, MSG, NAB, NAS, NAU, NCV, NEB, NET, NIrV, NIV, NJB, NLT, NRS, NWT, Phi, REB, RSV, TCW, TNIV, WNT

WHAT'S MISSING?
CHRIST ALONE SHED HIS BLOOD
TO PAY FOR OUR SINS

> Colossians 1:14 In whom we have redemption ~~through his blood~~, *even* the forgiveness of sins:

Remember what Hebrews 9:22 says:

> And almost all things are by the law purged with blood; and without shedding of blood is no remission (forgiveness of sin).

We cannot be forgiven without the shedding of blood. This is the same thing God wrote through Paul in Ephesians 1:7. We have a consistent God; and His scriptures are clear and consistent, too.

Missing from: *AMP*, Bar, BBE, CEV, CJB, CSB, DBY, ERV, ESV, GNB, GWN, HNV, ICB, ISV, JB, MOF, MRC, MSG, NAB, NAS, NAU, NCV, NEB, NET, NIrV, NIV, NJB, NLT, NRS, NWT, Phi, REB, RSV, TCW, TNIV, WEB, WNT

ക്ക ക്ക ക്ക

> Hebrews 1:3 Who being the brightness of *his* glory, and the express image of his person, and upholding all things by the word of his power, when he had ~~by himself~~ purged our sins, sat down on the right hand of the Majesty on high;

"By himself" means nothing else and no one else purged our sins. Only Jesus —not Mary, saints, angels, or anyone else— paid the price for our sins.

Missing from: *AMP*, ASV, Bar, CEV, CSB, *DBY*, DRA, ERV, ESV, GNB, GWN, ICB, ISV, JB, LB,

MOF, MRC, MSG, NAB, NAS, NAU, NCV, NEB,
NET, NIrV, NIV, NJB, NLT, NRS, NWT, REB,
RSV, TCW, TNIV, WNT

WHAT'S MISSING?
CHRIST'S BLOOD OF THE "NEW" TESTAMENT

Matthew 26:28 For this is my blood of the
~~new~~ testament, which is shed for many for the
remission of sins.

This isn't just any testament or covenant – it is the *New*
Testament promised to Israel in Jeremiah 31:31-34. [200]

Missing from: *AMP*, ASV, BBE, CEV, CJB, CSB,
DBY, ERV, ESV, GNB, GWN, JB, MRC, NAB,
NAS, NAU, NEB, NET, NIV, NJB, NLT, NRS,
NWT, REB, RSV, TCW, TNIV, WNT

෨   ෨   ෨

Mark 14:24 And he said unto them, This
is my blood of the ~~new~~ testament, which is
shed for many.

Missing from: *AMP*, ASV, BBE, CEV, CSB, *DBY,*
ERV, ESV, GNB, GWN, ISV, JB, MOF, NAB, NAS,
NAU, NEB, NET, NIV, NJB, NLT, NRS, NWT,
REB, RSV, TCW[201], TNIV, WNT

WHAT'S MISSING? THAT WE ARE NOT
SAVED BY WORKS OR RICHES

Mark 10:24 And the disciples were astonished at his words. But Jesus answereth again,
and saith unto them, Children, how hard is it
~~for them that trust in riches~~ to enter into the
kingdom of God.

---

200) See 1 Corinthians 11:25; 2 Corinthians 3:6; Hebrews 8:8-13; and 9:15-17.
201) TCW removes "new," then strangely changes it to "the covenant my Father
and I made from the beginning," a reading found in *no* Greek manuscripts.

When you remove these words, it teaches the false doctrine that it is difficult to enter the kingdom of God. Jesus called us to Himself, saying, "…my yoke *is* easy, and my burden is light" (See Matthew 11:28-30).

Missing from: *AMP*, Bar, CEV, CJB, CSB, ESV, GNB, GWN, ICB, JB, MRC, MSG, NAB, NAS, NAU, NCV, NEB, NET, NIrV, NIV, NJB, NLT, NRS, NWT, Phi, REB, RSV, TNIV

Romans 11:6 And if by grace, then *is it* no more of works: otherwise grace is no more grace. ~~But if *it be* of works, then is it no more grace: otherwise work is no more work~~.

This is one of the clearest statements in the Bible about salvation by grace, not by works. You cannot earn grace. Grace is by definition given freely by God. If works, you earned it yourself. And you can't be saved partly by grace and partly by works. It is one or the other.

Why would anyone remove this, unless their religion wanted to threaten people by making them "earn" their way into heaven?

Missing from: AMP, ASV, Bar, BBE, CEV, CJB, CSB, DBY, DRA, ERV, ESV, GNB, GWN, ICB, ISV, JB, LB, MOF, MRC, MSG, NAB, NAS, NAU, NCV, NEB, NET, NIrV, NIV, NJB, NLT, NRS, NWT, Phi, REB, RSV, TCW, TNIV, WNT

WHAT'S MISSING? REPENTANCE

Matthew 9:13 But go ye and learn what *that* meaneth, I will have mercy, and not sacrifice: for I am not come to call the righteous, but sinners ~~to repentance~~.

In this verse and Mark 2:17, Jesus doesn't just call sinners to Himself. He calls them to *repent*.

> Missing from: [AMP], ASV, Bar, BBE, CEV, CJB, CSB, DBY, DRA, ERV, ESV, GNB, GWN, ICB, ISV, JB, LB, MRC, MSG, MOF, NAB, NAS, NAU, NCV, NEB, NET, NIrV[202], NIV, NJB, NLT, NRS, NWT, Phi, REB, RSV, TCW, TNIV, WNT

WHAT'S MISSING?
DETAILS OF CHRIST'S MISSION

> Matthew 18:11 ~~For the Son of man is come to save that which was lost~~.

This is a key verse that explains Christ's real reason for coming to earth. Why is it missing in Alexandrian Bibles?

> Missing from: *AMP*, *ASV*, Bar, BBE, CEV, CJB, [CSB], ERV, ESV, GNB, GWN, ICB, JB, *MRC*, MOF, MSG, NAB, [NAS], [NAU], NCV, NEB, NET, NIrV, NIV, NJB, NLT, NRS, NWT, Phi, RSV, TNIV, WNT

ഀ   ഀ   ഀ

> Matthew 20:22 But Jesus answered and said, Ye know not what ye ask. Are ye able to drink of the cup that I shall drink of**,** ~~and to be baptized with the baptism that I am baptized with~~? They say unto him, We are able.

The Lord Jesus is about to give Himself as the ultimate sacrifice. God the Son is about to endure what no man could ever endure. Christ's sacrifice is far more than "drinking a cup," He is about to take on himself not only physical

---

202) In Matthew 9:13 and Mark 2:17, the NIrV took away the whole point, "to repentance," but added to scripture words that don't appear in any Greek text: "to follow me."

pain and suffering, but endure the punishment for every one of our sins.

How dare the translators remove so vivid an image as the "baptism of suffering!" No one was able to do what Christ did for us.

Missing from: *AMP*, ASV, Bar, BBE, CEV, CJB, CSB, DBY, DRA, ERV, ESV, GNB, GWN, ICB, JB, LB, MRC, MOF, MSG, NAB, NAS, NAU, NCV, NEB, NET, NIrV, NIV, NJB, NLT, NRS, Phi, REB, RSV, TNIV, WNT

Mark 3:15 And to have power ~~to heal sicknesses, and~~ to cast out devils:

Christ's miracles involved both healing the sick and casting out devils. Why did Alexandrians remove healing?

Missing from: *AMP*, ASV, Bar, BBE, CEV, CJB, CSB, *DBY,* ERV, ESV, GNB, GWN, ICB, ISV, JB, LB, MOF, MRC, MSG, NAB, NAS, NAU, NCV, NEB, NET, NIrV, NIV, NJB, NLT, NRS, NWT, Phi, REB, RSV, TNIV, WNT

Mark 10:21 Then Jesus beholding him loved him, and said unto him, One thing thou lackest: go thy way, sell whatsoever thou hast, and give to the poor, and thou shalt have treasure in heaven: and come, ~~take up the cross,~~ and follow me.

The rich man was used to "counting the cost." So Jesus spelled it out for him. It would cost him his life. Ask yourself: Why would somebody remove those crucial words?

Missing from: AMP, ASV, Bar, BBE, CEV, CJB, CSB, *DBY,* DRA, ERV, ESV, GNB, GWN, ICB, ISV, JB,

LB, MRC, MSG, NAB, NAS, NAU, NCV, NEB, NET, NIrV, NIV, NJB, NLT, NRS, NWT, Phi, REB, RSV, TCW, TNIV, WNT

Luke 4:18 The Spirit of the Lord is upon me, because he hath anointed me to preach the gospel to the poor; he hath sent me ~~to heal the brokenhearted~~, to preach deliverance to the captives, and recovering of sight to the blind, to set at liberty them that are bruised,

What a comfort to those with broken hearts. Why give so much "weight" to the few Alexandrian manuscripts that remove these words, over the piles of manuscripts that preserved them?

Missing from: AMP, ASV, Bar, CEV, CJB, CSB, DBY, ERV, ESV, GNB, GWN, ICB, ISV, JB, MOF, MRC, MSG, NAB, NAS, NAU, NCV, NEB, NET, NIrV, NIV, NJB, NLT, NRS, NWT, Phi, REB, RSV, TNIV, WNT

Luke 9:54-56 – Christ's purpose on earth [203]

Luke 9:54 And when his disciples James and John saw *this*, they said, Lord, wilt thou that we command fire to come down from heaven, and consume them, ~~even as Elias did~~?

Missing from: *AMP*, ASV, Bar, BBE, CEV, CJB, CSB, DRA, ERV, ESV, GNB, GWN, ICB, JB, LB, MOF, MRC, MSG, NAB, NAS, NAU, NCV, NEB, NET, NIrV, NIV, NJB, NLT, NRS, NWT, Phi, REB, RSV, TNIV, WNT

Luke 9:55 But he turned, and rebuked them,

---

203) See Chapter 3

and said, ~~Ye know not what manner of spirit ye are of~~.

Missing from: *AMP*, ASV, Bar, BBE, CEV, CJB, CSB, *DBY,* ERV, ESV, GNB, GWN, ICB, ISV, JB, LB, *MRC,* MSG, MOF, NAB, [NAS], [NAU], NCV, NEB, NET, NIrV, NIV, NJB, NLT, NRS, NWT, Phi, REB, RSV, TNIV, WNT

Luke 9:56 ~~For the Son of man is not come to destroy men's lives, but to save *them*~~. And they went to another village.

Missing from: *AMP*, ASV, Bar, BBE, CEV, CJB, CSB, DBY, ERV, ESV, GNB, GWN, ICB, ISV, JB, LB, MSG, MOF, NAB, [NAS], [NAU], NCV, NEB, NET, NIrV, NIV, NJB, NLT, NRS, NWT, Phi, REB, RSV, TNIV, WNT

What's Missing? Other Gospel Doctrines

Matthew 20:16 So the last shall be first, and the first last: ~~for many be called, but few chosen~~.

Missing from: *AMP*, ASV, Bar, BBE, CEV, CJB, CSB, ERV, ESV, GNB, GWN, ICB, JB, LB, MRC, MOF, MSG, NAB, NAS, NAU, NCV, NEB, NET, NIrV, NIV, NJB, NLT, NRS, NWT, Phi, REB, RSV, TCW, TNIV, WNT

Romans 10:15 And how shall they preach, except they be sent? as it is written, How beautiful are the feet of them that ~~preach the gospel of peace~~, and bring glad tidings of good things!

It's nice to hear "glad tidings." But it's *life or death* to hear "the gospel of peace" preached. It is a serious thing where the Alexandrians took out "gospel."

Missing from: AMP, ASV, Bar, BBE, CEV, CJB, CSB, ERV, ESV, GNB, GWN, ICB, ISV, JB, MOF, MRC, MSG, NAB, NAS, NAU, NCV, NEB, NET, NIrV, NIV, NJB, NLT, NRS, NWT, Phi, REB, RSV, TNIV, WNT

૭૦   ૭૦   ૭૦

Romans 15:29 And I am sure that, when I come unto you, I shall come in the fulness of the blessing ~~of the gospel~~ of Christ.

Missing from: *AMP*, ASV, Bar, BBE, CEV, CJB, CSB, DBY, ERV, ESV, GNB, GWN, ICB, ISV, JB, LB, MOF, MRC, MSG, NAB, NAS, NAU, NCV, NEB, NET, NIrV, NIV, NJB, NLT, NRS, NWT, Phi, REB, RSV, TNIV, WNT

MISSING WORDS CONCERNING SALVATION AND DAMNATION

Mark 2:17 When Jesus heard it, he saith unto them, They that are whole have no need of the physician, but they that are sick: I came not to call the righteous, but sinners ~~to repentance~~.

Missing from: AMP, ASV, Bar, BBE, CEV, CJB, CSB, DBY, DRA, ERV, ESV, GNB, GWN, ICB, ISV, JB, MOF, MRC, MSB, NAB, NAS, NAU, NCV, NEB, NET, NIrV, NIV, NJB, NLT, NRS, NWT, Phi, REB, RSV, TCW, TNIV, WNT

WHAT'S MISSING? WORDS REGARDING HELL

Mark 9:44 ~~Where their worm dieth not, and the fire is not quenched~~.

Every word in the Bible is important. But if it is repeated, pay attention. If it is repeated three or four times, *watch out.* God is making sure we never forget the lesson.

That is why it is so sinful that Alexandrians and others took away what God repeated —even to the point of deleting whole phrases and verses.

Missing from: AMP, *ASV*, Bar, BBE, CEV, CJB, [CSB], *DBY*, ERV, ESV, GNB, GWN, ICB, JB, LB, MOF, *MRC*, MSG, NAB, [NAS], [NAU], NCV, NEB, NET, NIrV, NIV, NJB, NLT, NRS, NWT, Phi, REB, RSV, TNIV, WNT

❧   ❧   ❧

Mark 9:45 And if thy foot offend thee, cut it off: it is better for thee to enter halt into life, than having two feet to be cast into hell, ~~into the fire that never shall be quenched~~:

Missing from: AMP, ASV, Bar, BBE, CEV, CJB, [CSB], ERV, ESV, GNB, GWN, ICB, ISV, JB, LB, MOF, MRC, MSG, NAB, NAS, NAU, NCV, NET, NIrV, NIV, NJB, NLT, NRS, NWT, Phi, REB, RSV, TCW, TNIV, WNT

❧   ❧   ❧

Mark 9:46 ~~Where their worm dieth not, and the fire is not quenched~~.

Missing from: AMP, *ASV*, Bar, BBE, CEV, CJB, [CSB], *DBY*, ERV, ESV, GNB, GWN, ICB, JB, LB, MOF, *MRC*, MSG, NAB, [NAS], [NAU], NCV, NEB, NET, NIrV, NIV, NJB, NLT, NRS, NWT, Phi, REB, RSV, TNIV, WNT

WHAT'S MISSING:
WORDS REGARDING THE SECOND COMING

Matthew 25:13   Watch therefore, for ye

know neither the day nor the hour ~~wherein the Son of man cometh~~.

Missing from: *AMP*, ASV, Bar, BBE, CJB, CSB, DBY, DRA, ERV, ESV, GNB, GWN, ISV, JB, LB[204], MRC, MOF, NAB, NAS, NAU, NEB, NET, NIrV[205], NIV, NJB, NLT, NRS, NWT, Phi, REB, RSV, TNIV, WNT

WHAT'S MISSING: WORDS REGARDING THE RESURRECTION OF THE DEAD

Mark 12:23 In the resurrection therefore, ~~when they shall rise~~, whose wife shall she be of them? for the seven had her to wife.

Missing from: AMP, ASV, CJB, ERV, ISV, LB, (NAB), NIV, NLT, RSV, NRS, NWT, LB, TNIV, WNT

The following versions combine the two phrases into one, eliminating the big word "resurrection:"

BBE, CEV, GWN, ICB, MOF, NIrV, NCV, TCW

Acts 24:15 And have hope toward God, which they themselves also allow, that there shall be a resurrection ~~of the dead~~, both of the just and unjust.

Missing from: AMP, ASV, Bar, BBE[206], CEV, CJB, CSB, DBY, DRA, ERV, ESV, GWN, ICB, JB, LB, MOF, NAB, NAS, NAU, NCV, NEB, NET, NIrV, NIV, NJM, NLT, NRS, NWT, Phi, REB, RSV, TNIV

---

204) The LB merely summarizes, "of my return."
205) The NIrV amazingly not only *takes away* "the Son of man." It also *adds* "the groom" in its place, a reading which does not exist in any Greek text, anywhere.
206) The BBE, CEV, ICB, NCV and NIrV actually do the opposite: each combines the two phrases into one, taking away the big word "resurrection."

WHAT'S MISSING? WORDS REGARDING THE JUDGMENT AND ETERNAL PUNISHMENT

Matthew 5:22 But I say unto you, That whosoever is angry with his brother ~~without a cause~~ shall be in danger of the judgment: and whosoever shall say to his brother, Raca, shall be in danger of the council: but whosoever shall say, Thou fool, shall be in danger of hell fire.

It is not merely being *angry* that makes us in danger of the judgment. Bibles that remove "without a cause" make Jesus "in danger of the judgment," because He was angry when he cleansed the Temple —twice. [207]

Missing from: AMP, ASV, Bar, BBE, CEV, CJB, CSB, DBY, DRA, ERV, ESV, GNB, GWN, ICB, JB, LB, MSG, MOF, NAS, NAU, NCV, NEB, NET, NIrV, NIV, NJB, NLT, NRS, NWT, Phi, REB, RSV, TCW, TNIV, WNT

෧ ෧ ෧

Matthew 21:44 ~~And whosoever shall fall on this stone shall be broken: but on whomsoever it shall fall, it will grind him to powder~~.

It's Jesus Christ, or the judgment without Christ. It doesn't get much plainer than this.

Missing from: *AMP*, CJB, [CSB], GNB, JB, (NAB), NEB, NIV, NJB, NRS, (Phi), REB, RSV

෧ ෧ ෧

Matthew 23:14 ~~Woe unto you, scribes and Pharisees, hypocrites! for ye devour widows' houses, and for a pretence make long prayer:~~

---

207) See John 2:13-17; Matthew 21:12-13; and Mark 11:15-18.

~~therefore ye shall receive the greater damnation.~~

Those who don't put their faith in Christ will not be saved. They will be judged by their works (Revelation 20:13).

But this verse says that religious leaders, who should know better and should be examples to the people, will be judged more harshly and shall receive "the greater damnation."

Missing from: *AMP*, *ASV*, Bar, BBE, CEV, CJB, [CSB], DBY, ERV, ESV, GNB, *ISV*, GWN, ICB, JB, *MRC*, MOF, MSG, NAB, [NAS], [NAU], NCV, NEB, NET, NIrV, NIV, NJB, NLT, NRS, NWT, Phi, REB, RSV, TNIV, WNT

෨ ෨ ෨

Mark 6:11 And whosoever shall not receive you, nor hear you, when ye depart thence, shake off the dust under your feet for a testimony against them. ~~Verily I say unto you, It shall be more tolerable for Sodom and Gomorrha in the day of judgment, than for that city.~~

Missing from: *AMP*, ASV, Bar, BBE, CEV, CJB, CSB, DBY, DRA, ERV, ESV, GNB, GWN, ICB, ISV, JB, LB, MOF, MRC, MSG, NAB, NAS, NAU, NCV, NEB, NET, NIrV, NIV, NJB, NLT, NRS, NWT, Phi, REB, RSV, TCW[208], TNIV, WNT

---

208) TCW mentions "Sodom and Gomorrha," but says nothing about the Day of Judgment.

MISSING WORDS CONCERNING HEAVEN AND ANGELS

WHAT'S MISSING?
WORDS CONCERNING HEAVEN

> John 3:13 And no man hath ascended up to heaven, but he that came down from heaven, *even* the Son of man ~~which is in heaven~~.

This verse doesn't only concern "heaven." It also teaches us the fact that Jesus is both divine and human at the same time. So while God's Son lived on earth, Jesus was *at the same time* in heaven.

> Missing from: *AMP*, Bar[209], BBE, CEV, CJB, CSB, ESV, GNB, GWN, ICB, LB, MOF, MRC,MSG, NAB, NAS, NAU, NCV, NEB[210], NET, NIrV, NIV, NJB, NLT, NRS, NWT, Phi, RSV, TCW[211], TNIV, WNT[212]

❧   ❧   ❧

> John 17:12 While I was with them ~~in the world~~, I kept them in thy name: those that thou gavest me I have kept, and none of them is lost, but the son of perdition; that the scripture might be fulfilled.

While heaven is not named, the fact that Jesus specified the time he was with the disciples "in the world" adds weight to the fact that He is also from heaven.

---

209) Barclay (Bar) removes "which *is* in heaven" and changes it to "who *comes from* heaven," which doesn't exist in *any* Greek text *anywhere*.
210) The NEB copies Weymouth (WNT), removing "which *is* in heaven" and changing it to "whose *home* is in heaven."
211) TCW removes "which *is* in heaven" and changes it to "before He was born" – hiding the fact that Jesus is God, in heaven and on earth at the same time.
212) The WNT removes "which *is* in heaven" and changes it to "whose *home* is in heaven."

Missing from: AMP, ASV, Bar, BBE, CEV, CJB, CSB, DBY, DRA, ERV, ESV, GNB, GWN, ICB, ISV, JB, LB, MOF, MRC, MSG, NAB, NAS, NAU, NCV, NEB, NET, NIrV, NIV, NJB, NLT, NRS, NWT, Phi, REB, RSV, TNIV, WNT

❧   ❧   ❧

Hebrews 10:34   For ye had compassion of me in my bonds, and took joyfully the spoiling of your goods, knowing in yourselves that ye have ~~in heaven~~ a better and an enduring substance.

God isn't promising us blessings in the here and now only. We have something so much better waiting for us in heaven.

Missing from: AMP, ASV, Bar, BBE, CEV, CJB, CSB, DBY, DRA, ERV, ESV, GNB, GWN, ICB, ISV, JB, MOF, MSG, NAB, NAS, NAU, NCV, NET, NIrV, NIV, NJB, NLT, NRS, NWT, Phi, REB, RSV, TNIV, WNT

❧   ❧   ❧

Revelation 16:17   And the seventh angel poured out his vial into the air; and there came a great voice out of the temple ~~of heaven~~, from the throne, saying, It is done.

Missing from: *AMP*, ASV, Bar, BBE, CEV, CJB, CSB, DRA, ERV, ESV, GNB, GWN, ICB, ISV, JB, MRC, MSG, NAB, NAS, NAU, NCV, NEB, NET, NIrV, NIV, NJB, NLT, NRS, NWT, Phi, REB, RSV, TNIV, WNT

WHAT'S MISSING?
WORDS ABOUT DOCTRINES OF ANGELS

ANGELS OF GOD

Matthew 22:30 For in the resurrection they neither marry, nor are given in marriage, but are as the angels ~~of God~~ in heaven.

There are two kinds of angels: of God and of the devil. This verse really only talks about the angels of God.

Missing from: AMP, ASV, Bar, BBE, CEV, CJB, CSB, ERV, ESV, GNB, GWN, ICB, ISV, JB, LB, MRC, NAB, NAS, NAU, NCV, NEB, NET, NIrV, NIV, NJB, NLT, NRS, NWT, Phi, REB, RSV, TCW, TNIV, WNT

ॐ ॐ ॐ

Matthew 25:31 When the Son of man shall come in his glory, and all the ~~holy~~ angels with him, then shall he sit upon the throne of his glory:

Angels of God are *holy*, meaning set apart completely for God.

Missing from: *AMP*, ASV, Bar, BBE, CEV, CJB, CSB, DBY, DRA, ERV, ESV, GNB, GWN, ICB, ISV, JB, LB, MRC, MOF, MSG, NAB, NAS, NAU, NCV, NEB, NET, NIrV, NIV, NJB, NLT, NRS, NWT, Phi, REB, RSV, TCW, TNIV, WNT

ॐ ॐ ॐ

Luke 22:43 ~~And there appeared an angel unto him from heaven, strengthening him.~~

Only a few versions take this out or call it "not scripture." Why did *these*?

Missing from: [CSB], (NAB), Phi, RSV ·

❧　　❧　　❧

John 5:4 ~~For an angel went down at a certain season into the pool, and troubled the water: whosoever then first after the troubling of the water stepped in was made whole of whatsoever disease he had~~.

The story of John 5 makes no sense when this verse is removed. So why did the Alexandrians remove it?

Missing from: *AMP*, Bar, ASV, BBE, CEV, CJB, [CSB], *DBY*, ERV, ESV, GNB, GWN, ICB, (LB), [MOF], MSG, NAB, [NAS], [NAU], NCV, NEB, NET, NIrV, NIV, NJB, NLT, NRS, NWT, (Phi), REB, RSV, TNIV, WNT

❧　　❧　　❧

Acts 7:30 And when forty years were expired, there appeared to him in the wilderness of mount Sina an angel ~~of the Lord~~ in a flame of fire in a bush.

An "angel *of the Lord*" is a very special angel. It is a messenger that represents the Lord God Himself when talking to humans.

Missing from: AMP, ASV, Bar, BBE, CEV, CJB, CSB, DBY, DRA, ERV, ESV, GNB, GWN, ICB, ISV, JB, LB, MRC, MSG, NAB, NAS, NAU, NCV, NEB, NET, NIrV, NIV, NJB, NLT, NRS, NWT, Phi, REB, RSV, TCW[213], TNIV, WNT

❧　　❧　　❧

Colossians 2:18 Let no man beguile you of your reward in a voluntary humility and

---

213) TCW *totally changes* this verse, removing "an angel of the Lord" and inserting "God" in its place.

worshipping of angels, intruding into those things which he hath ~~not~~ seen, vainly puffed up by his fleshly mind,

By removing one word, modern Bible versions created a complete contradiction. Either the person *has* seen or he has *not* seen. It has to be one or the other. Both cannot be right.

Missing from: AMP, ASV, BBE, CJB, ERV, GWN, ICB, ISV, JB, LB, MRC, NAS, NAU, NET, NIrV, NIV, NJB, NLT, NWT, Phi, TNIV,

What's missing: the entire concept of "things which he hath not seen," usually in paraphrases.

Missing from: Bar, CEV, CSB, ESV, GNB, MOF, MSG, NAB, NEB, NRS, REB, RSV, NCV, TCW, WNT

SATAN

Luke 4:8 And Jesus answered and said unto him, ~~Get thee behind me, Satan~~: for it is written, Thou shalt worship the Lord thy God, and him only shalt thou serve.

Missing from: *AMP*, ASV, Bar, BBE, CEV, CJB, CSB, DBY, DRA, ERV, ESV, GNB, GWN, ICB, ISV, JB, LB, MOF, MRC, MSG, NAB, NAS, NAU, NCV, NEB, NET, NIrV, NIV, NJB, NLT, NRS, NWT, Phi, REB, RSV, TNIV, WNT

MISSING WORDS CONCERNING PRAYER AND FASTING

Mark 13:33 Take ye heed, watch ~~and pray~~: for ye know not when the time is.

Jesus made it clear: it is not enough just to "watch." We have to *pray* as well.

Missing from: *AMP*, Bar, CEV, CJB, CSB, ESV, GNB, GWN, ICB, ISV, JB, LB, MRC, MSG, NAB, NAS, NAU, NET, NCV, NEB, NIrV, NIV, NJB, NLT, NRS, NWT, Phi, REB, RSV, TNIV

ও   ও   ও

Mark 9:29 And he said unto them, This kind can come forth by nothing, but by prayer ~~and fasting~~.

Did the Alexandrians have a problem with fasting?

Missing from: *AMP*, Bar, ASV, BBE, CEV, CJB, [CSB], ERV, ESV, GNB, GWN, ICB, JB, LB, MRC, MSG, NAB, NAS, NAU, NCV, NEB, NET, NIrV, NIV, NJB, NLT, NRS, NWT, Phi, REB, RSV, TCW[214], TNIV, WNT

ও   ও   ও

Acts 10:30 And Cornelius said, Four days ago I was ~~fasting~~ until this hour; ~~and~~ at the ninth hour I prayed in my house, and, behold, a man stood before me in bright clothing,

In order to take these words out of the text, they had to completely reword Cornelius' testimony. Check any of the Bibles listed and see for yourself.

Missing from: AMP, ASV, Bar, BBE, CEV, CJB, CSB, *DBY*, DRA, ERV, ESV, GNB, GWN, ICB, ISV, JB, LB, MOF, MRC, MSG, NAB, NAS, NAU, NCV, NEB, NET, NIrV, NIV, NJB, NLT, NRS, NWT, Phi, REB, RSV, TNIV, WNT

ও   ও   ও

1 Corinthians 7:5 Defraud ye not one the

---

214) TCW removes "fasting" and adds "walking humbly with God" —found in no Greek manuscript, anywhere. This is also strangely added in Matthew 17:21.

other, except *it be* with consent for a time, that ye may give yourselves to ~~fasting and~~ prayer; and come together again, that Satan tempt you not for your incontinency.

Since this concerns a successful married life, it is amazing that anyone would want to read a Bible with this important element removed.

Missing from: AMP, ASV, Bar, BBE, CEV, CJB, CSB, DBY, DRA, ERV, ESV, GNB, GWN, ICB, ISV, JB, LB, MOF, MRC, NAB, NAS, NAU, NCV, NEB, NET, NIrV, NIV, NJB, NLT, NRS, NWT, Phi, REB, RSV, TNIV, WNT

Matthew 17:21 ~~Howbeit this kind goeth not out but by prayer and fasting~~.

The fact that some devils only come out by prayer and fasting is something I would want to know. What kind of person would remove these words of Jesus?

Missing from: *AMP, ASV, Bar,* BBE, CJB, [CSB], ERV, ICB, JB, MOF, NAB, [NAS], [NAU], NCV, NEB, NET, NIrV, NIV, NJB, NLT, NRS, NWT, Phi, REB, RSV, TNIV

OTHER MISSING WORDS OF CHRIST

You don't have to go to the Middle East on a quest for the "missing words of Christ" on some ancient scroll. You can find them right in the King James Bible. Jesus actually spoke these words. How dare anyone take them away. *Every* word of my Lord is sacred and holy.

Here are some more examples of what's missing from the so-called "modern Bibles."

Matthew 5:44 But I say unto you, Love your enemies, ~~bless them that curse you, do good to them that hate you~~, and pray for them which ~~despitefully use you, and~~ persecute you;

Missing from: AMP, ASV, Bar, BBE, CEV, CJB, CSB, *DBY*, DRA,[215] ERV, ESV, GNB, GWN, ICB, ISV, JB, LB, MRC, MSG, MOF, NAB, NAS, NAU, NCV, NEB, NET, NIrV, NIV, NJB, NLT, NRS, NWT, Phi, REB, RSV, TCW, TNIV, WNT

Matthew 6:13 And lead us not into temptation, but deliver us from evil: ~~For thine is the kingdom, and the power, and the glory, for ever. Amen~~.

Missing from: *AMP*, ASV, Bar, BBE, CEV, CJB, [CSB], DBY, DRA, ERV, ESV, GNB, GWN, ICB, ISV, JB, LB, *MRC*, MOF, NAB, [NAS], [NAU], NCV, NEB, NET, NIrV, NIV, NJB, NLT, NRS, NWT, Phi, REB, RSV, TNIV, WNT

Matthew 12:35 A good man out of the good treasure ~~of the heart~~ bringeth forth good things: and an evil man out of the evil treasure bringeth forth evil things.

Missing from: ASV, Bar, BBE, CJB, CSB, DBY, DRA, ERV, ESV, GNB, GWN, HNV, ISV, JB, MSG, MOF, NAB, NAS, NAU, NET, NIrV, NIV, NJB, NRS, NWT, REB, RSV, WEB, TNIV, WNT

Matthew 15:6 And honour not his father

---

215) DRA removes "bless them that curse you" only.

~~or his mother~~, he shall be free. Thus have ye made the commandment of God of none effect by your tradition.

Missing from: *AMP*, ASV, Bar, BBE, CSB, ERV, ESV, GNB, GWN, ICB, ISV, NAB, NET, NIV, NRS, RSV, WNT

Matthew 15:8   This people ~~draweth nigh unto me with their mouth, and~~ honoureth me with *their* lips; but their heart is far from me.

Missing from: *AMP*, Bar, BBE, CEV, CSB, DBY, DRA, ESV, GNB, GWN, ICB, ISV, JB, LB, MRC, MOF, MSG, NAS, NAU, NCV, NEB, NIrV, NIV, NRS, REB, RSV, TNIV, WNT

Matthew 16:2-3[216]   He answered and said unto them, ~~When it is evening, ye say, It will be fair weather: for the sky is red. And in the morning, It will be foul weather to day: for the sky is red and lowring. O ye hypocrites, ye can discern the face of the sky; but can ye not discern the signs of the times?~~

Missing from: *AMP*, MOF, NEB, REB

Matthew 16:3   And in the morning, It will be foul weather to day: for the sky is red and lowring. ~~O ye hypocrites~~, ye can discern the face of the sky; but can ye not discern the signs of the times?

---

216) See Chapter 6 about Matthew 16:2-3.

Missing from: AMP, ASV, Bar, BBE, CEV, CJB, CSB, DBY, DRA, ERV, ESV, GNB, GWN, ICB, ISV, JB, LB, MRC, MSG, NAB, NAS, NAU, NCV, NET, NIrV, NIV, NJB, NLT, NRS, NWT, Phi, RSV, TCW, TNIV, WNT

❧   ❧   ❧

Matthew 19:9 And I say unto you, Whosoever shall put away his wife, except it be for fornication, and shall marry another, committeth adultery: ~~and whoso marrieth her which is put away doth commit adultery~~.

Missing from: *AMP*, Bar, CEV, CJB, CSB, ESV, GNB, GWN, ICB, ISV, JB, LB, MRC, MSG, NAB, NAS, NAU, NCV, NEB, NET, NIrV, NIV, NJB, NLT, NRS, NWT, Phi, REB, RSV, TNIV, WNT

❧   ❧   ❧

Matthew 20:7 They say unto him, Because no man hath hired us. He saith unto them, Go ye also into the vineyard; ~~and whatsoever is right, that shall ye receive~~.

Missing from: *AMP*, ASV, Bar, BBE, CEV, CJB, CSB, *DBY*, DRA, ERV, ESV, GNB, GWN, ICB, ISV, JB, LB, MRC, MOF, MSG, NAB, NAS, NAU, NCV, NEB, NET, NIrV, NIV, NJB, NLT, NRS, NWT, Phi, REB, RSV, TNIV, WNT

❧   ❧   ❧

Matthew 24:7 For nation shall rise against nation, and kingdom against kingdom: and there shall be famines, ~~and pestilences~~, and earthquakes, in divers places.

Missing from: AMP, Bar, ASV, BBE, CEV, CJB, CSB, ERV, ESV, GNB, GWN, ICB, ISV, JB, LB, MRC, MOF, MSG, NAB, NAS, NAU, NCV, NEB, NET,

NIrV, NIV, NJB, NLT, NRS, NWT, Phi, REB, RSV, TNIV, WNT

Mark 4:11 And he said unto them, Unto you it is given ~~to know~~ the mystery of the kingdom of God: but unto them that are without, all these things are done in parables:

False Bibles give the impression that the only thing the disciples have is "the mystery" – but Christians are able to *know* the mystery – all the pieces of the puzzle make sense for the Christian.

Missing from: AMP, ASV, BBE, CEV, CJB, CSB, *DBY*, ERV, ESV, GNB, GWN, HNV, ISV, JB, MOF, MRC, MSG[217], NAB, NAS, NAU, NEB, NET, NIrV, NIV, NJB, NRS, NWT, Phi, REB, RSV, TNIV, WEB, WNT

Mark 7:16 ~~If any man have ears to hear, let him hear~~.

Missing from: *AMP, ASV*, Bar, BBE, CEV, CJB, ERV, ESV, GNB, ICB, LB, *MRC*, MSG, NAB, [NAS], [NAU], NCV, NEB, NET, NIrV, NIV, NLT, NRS, NWT, Phi, REB, RSV, TNIV, WNT

Mark 8:26 And he sent him away to his house, saying, Neither go into the town, ~~nor tell it to any in the town~~.

Missing from: *AMP*, Bar, ASV, BBE, CEV, CJB, CSB, ERV, ESV, GNB, GWN, ICB, JB, LB, MOF, MRC,

---

217) The MSG simply summarizes with the word "insight" and removes "to know the mystery."

MSG, NAB, NAS, NAU, NCV, NEB[218], NET, NIrV, NIV, NJB, NLT, NRS, NWT, Phi, REB, RSV, TNIV, WNT

Mark 9:42 And whosoever shall offend one of these little ones that believe ~~in me~~, it is better for him that a millstone were hanged about his neck, and he were cast into the sea.

Missing from: CEV[219], *DBY*, JB, MOF, MSG, (NAB), NAS, NAU, NJB, NWT, REB, WNT

Mark 9:49 For every one shall be salted with fire, ~~and every sacrifice shall be salted with salt.~~

Missing from: AMP, ASV, BBE, CEV, CJB, CSB, ERV, ESV, GWN, ICB, JB, LB, MOF, MRC, MSG, NAB, NAS, NAU, NCV, NEB, NET, NIrV, NIV, NJB, NLT, NRS, NWT, Phi, REB, RSV, TNIV, WNT

Mark 11:26 ~~But if ye do not forgive, neither will your Father which is in heaven forgive your trespasses.~~

That is such an important doctrine to remember, I want it repeated in my Bible as often as the Lord Jesus said it. It is very sad that it was removed from all the Bible versions below:

Missing from: *AMP, ASV,* Bar, BBE, CEV, CJB, [CSB], ERV, ESV, GNB, GWN, ICB, JB, LB, MOF,

---

218) The NEB kept "nor tell it to any in the town," then removed "neither go into the town," though everyone else knows it belongs there.
219) The CEV removes the whole phrase "that believe in me" and substitutes "followers."

MRC, MSG, NAB, [NAS], [NAU], NCV, NEB, NET, NIrV, NIV, NJB, NLT, NRS, NWT, Phi, REB, RSV, TNIV, WNT

❧   ❧   ❧

Mark 12:30 And thou shalt love the Lord thy God with all thy heart, and with all thy soul, and with all thy mind, and with all thy strength: ~~this is the first commandment~~.

Missing from: *AMP*, ASV, Bar, BBE, CEV, CJB, CSB, ERV, ESV, GNB, GWN, ISV, JB, LB, MOF, MRC, MSG, NAB, NAS, NAU, NCV, NEB, NET, NIrV, NIV, NJB, NLT, NRS, NWT, Phi, REB, RSV, TNIV, WNT

❧   ❧   ❧

Mark 13:14 But when ye shall see the abomination of desolation, ~~spoken of by Daniel the prophet~~, standing where it ought not, (let him that readeth understand,) then let them that be in Judaea flee to the mountains:

Missing from: *AMP*, ASV, Bar, BBE, CEV, CJB, CSB, DBY, DRA, ERV, ESV, GNB, GWN, ICB[220], ISV, JB, LB, MOF, MRC, MSG, NAB, NAS, NAU, NCV, NEB, NET, NIrV[221], NIV, NJB, NLT, NRS, NWT, Phi, REB, RSV, TNIV, WNT

❧   ❧   ❧

Luke 11:11 If a son shall ask ~~bread~~ of any of you that is a father, ~~will he give him a stone?~~ or if he ask a fish, will he for a fish give him a serpent?

---

220) The ICB and NCV take away the reference to Daniel from scripture, and then add a footnote explaining where it is mentioned in Daniel.
221) The NIrV takes away the reference to Daniel from scripture, and then it adds in parentheses three scriptures Jesus is referring to from Daniel.

Missing from: *AMP*, Bar, CEV, CJB, CSB, ESV, GNB, GWN, ICB, MOF, MRC, MSG, NAB, NAS, NAU, NCV, NEB, NET, NIrV, NIV, NJB, NLT, NRS, NWT, Phi, REB, RSV, TNIV

ഔ ഔ ഔ

Luke 11:29 And when the people were gathered thick together, he began to say, This is an evil generation: they seek a sign; and there shall no sign be given it, but the sign of Jonas ~~the prophet~~.

Missing from: [AMP], ASV, Bar, BBE, CEV, CJB, CSB, DBY, ERV, ESV, GNB, GWN, ICB, ISV, JB, LB, MOF, MRC, MSG, NAB, NAS, NAU, NCV, NEB, NET, NIrV, NIV, NJB, NLT, NRS, NWT, Phi, REB, RSV, TCW, TNIV, WNT

ഔ ഔ ഔ

Luke 20:23 But he perceived their craftiness, and said unto them, ~~Why tempt ye me?~~

It is a major thing to try to tempt the Lord. So what made the Alexandrians think they could remove these words and get away with it? As Jesus spoke elsewhere, "Thou shalt not tempt the Lord thy God" (Matthew 4:7; Luke 4:12).

Missing from: AMP, ASV, Bar, BBE, CEV, CJB, CSB, ERV, ESV, GNB, GWN, ICB, ISV, JB, LB, MOF, MRC, MSG, NAB, NAS, NAU, NCV, NEB, NET, NIrV, NIV, NJB, NLT, NRS, NWT, Phi, REB, RSV, TCW, TNIV, WNT

ഔ ഔ ഔ

Luke 22:68 And if I also ask you, ye will not answer me, ~~nor let me go~~.

Missing from: AMP, ASV, Bar, BBE, CEV, CJB, CSB, ERV, ESV, GNB, GWN, ICB, ISV, JB, LB, MOF, MRC, MSG, NAB, NAS, NAU, NCV, NEB, NET,

NIrV, NIV, NJB, NLT, NRS, NWT, Phi, REB, RSV, TNIV, WNT

❧ ❧ ❧

Luke 24:36 And as they thus spake, Jesus himself stood in the midst of them, ~~and saith unto them, Peace be unto you~~.

Jesus' greeting was given to calm the disciples who were probably freaked out. Note that only a few Bibles had the nerve to remove these words of Christ.

Missing from: CEV, CJB, LB?[222], MRC, NAS, NEB, [[NWT]], RSV

❧ ❧ ❧

John 3:15 That whosoever believeth in him ~~should not perish, but~~ have eternal life.

This is a vital doctrine that needs to be repeated: those who do not believe in Jesus, God's Son, will perish. But so many Bibles take away words from clear verses like this. No wonder so many people refuse to believe in a future punishment of the wicked.

Missing from: *AMP*, ASV, Bar, BBE, CEV, CJB, CSB, *DBY*, ERV, ESV, GNB, GWN, ICB, ISV, JB, LB, MOF, MRC, NAB, NAS, NAU, NCV, NEB, NET, NIrV, NIV, NJB, NLT, NRS, NWT, Phi, REB, RSV, TCW, TNIV, WNT

❧ ❧ ❧

John 7:8 Go ye up unto this feast: I go not up ~~yet~~ unto this feast; for my time is not yet full come. (See Chapter 1)

Missing from: [AMP], ASV, CEV, DBY, DRA, ESV,

---

222) The LB summarizes that He "greeted them," but took away Jesus' actual words, "Peace be unto you."

GNB, JB, MOF, MRC, NAB, NAS, NAU, NEB, NET, NJB, NLT, NRS, REB, RSV, TNIV

❧   ❧   ❧

Revelation 2:15 So hast thou also them that hold the doctrine of the Nicolaitans, ~~which thing I hate~~.

Missing from: *AMP*, ASV, Bar, BBE, CEV, CJB, CSB, DBY, DRA, ERV, ESV, GNB, GWN, HNV, ICB, ISV, JB, LB, MOF, MRC, MSG, NAB, NAS, NAU, NCV, NEB, NET, NIrV, NIV, NJB, NLT, NRS, NWT, Phi, REB, RSV, TCW, TNIV, WEB, WNT

MISSING HISTORICAL DETAILS CONCERNING THE LIFE OF CHRIST AND THE EARLY CHURCH

The Alexandrians removed many, many details from their Bibles. Modern scholars pretend they're not important. Are they important or not? See for yourself.

WHAT'S MISSING?
DETAILS FROM THE LIFE OF CHRIST

Matthew 12:47 ~~Then one said unto him, Behold, thy mother and thy brethren stand without, desiring to speak with thee~~.

This verse is missing in both Sinaiticus and Vaticanus, yet most Bibles keep it in the text anyway. What hypocrites. Even Westcott and Hort put it in their Bible.

But it's obvious why these modern "scholars" were intimidated: this verse is in almost every other manuscript in history.

Missing from: CJB, JB, MOF, (NAB), RSV

❧   ❧   ❧

Matthew 27:24 When Pilate saw that he could prevail nothing, but that rather a tumult was made, he took water, and washed his hands before the multitude, saying, I am innocent of the blood of this ~~just~~ person: see ye to it.

Pilate saw Jesus as "just." That pronouncement alone should have cleared Jesus of all charges. But we all know that didn't happen. Read *The Illegal Trial of Jesus* by Wingo to learn about the many laws that were broken.

Missing from: *AMP*, Bar, CEV, CJB, CSB, ESV, GNB, GWN, ICB, ISV, JB, MRC, MSG, NAB, NAS, NAU, NCV, NEB, NET, NIrV, NIV, NJB, NLT, NRS, NWT, Phi, REB, RSV, TCW, TNIV, WNT

❧   ❧   ❧

Mark 1:14 Now after that John was put in prison, Jesus came into Galilee, preaching the gospel ~~of the kingdom~~ of God,

It wasn't just the "good news of God." It was the good news of the *kingdom* of God. By faith in Jesus Christ, we inherit the kingdom of God. Big difference, don't you think?

Missing from: *AMP*, ASV, Bar, BBE, CEV, CJB, CSB, ERV, ESV, GNB, GWN, ICB, JB, LB, MOF, MRC, MSG, NAB, NAS, NAU, NCV, NEB, NET, NIrV, NIV, NJB, NLT, NRS, NWT, Phi, REB, RSV, TNIV, WNT

❧   ❧   ❧

Mark 1:42 And ~~as soon as he had spoken,~~ immediately the leprosy departed from him, and he was cleansed.

Missing from: AMP, ASV, Bar, BBE, CEV, CJB, CSB, ERV, ESV, GNB, GWN, ICB, JB, LB, MRC, MSG, NAB, NAS, NAU, NCV, NEB, NET, NIrV, NIV, NJB, NLT, NRS, RSV, NWT, Phi, REB, TCW, TNIV, WNT

Mark 11:10 Blessed be the kingdom of our father David, that cometh ~~in the name of the Lord~~: Hosanna in the highest.

Missing from: AMP, ASV, Bar, BBE, CEV, CJB, CSB, DBY, DRA, ERV, ESV, GNB, GWN, ICB, ISV, JB, LB, MOF, MRC, MSG, NAB, NAS, NAU, NCV, NEB, NET, NIrV, NIV, NJB, NLT, NRS, NWT, Phi, REB, RSV, TNIV, WNT

Mark 14:68 But he denied, saying, I know not, neither understand I what thou sayest. And he went out into the porch; ~~and the cock crew~~.

The earlier edition of the NAS is missing these words; but the newer edition, the NAU, as well as most new versions, have them. That is because newer manuscript discoveries confirmed what the King James and other preserved Bibles had said all along.

Missing from: *AMP*, Bar, ICB, JB, MRC, (NAB), NAS, NEB, NIrV, NIV, NWT, REB, RSV, TNIV

Mark 15:28 ~~And the scripture was fulfilled, which saith, And he was numbered with the transgressors~~.

This is the *only* place in the whole Bible that states the fulfillment of this prophecy, found in Isaiah 53:12.

Missing from: *AMP*, *ASV*, Bar, BBE, CEV, CJB, [CSB], *DBY*, ERV, ESV, GNB, GWN, ICB, *ISV*, JB, MOF, *MRC*, MSG, NAB, [NAS], [NAU], NCV, NEB, NET, NIrV, NIV, NJB, NLT, NRS, NWT, Phi, REB, RSV, TNIV, WNT

❧   ❧   ❧

Mark 16:9-20 ~~Now when *Jesus* was risen early the first *day* of the week, he appeared first to Mary Magdalene, out of whom he had cast seven devils. *And* she went and told them that had been with him, as they mourned and wept. And they, when they had heard that he was alive, and had been seen of her, believed not. After that he appeared in another form unto two of them, as they walked, and went into the country. And they went and told *it* unto the residue: neither believed they them. Afterward he appeared unto the eleven as they sat at meat, and upbraided them with their unbelief and hardness of heart, because they believed not them which had seen him after he was risen. And he said unto them, Go ye into all the world, and preach the gospel to every creature. He that believeth and is baptized shall be saved; but he that believeth not shall be damned. And these signs shall follow them that believe; In my name shall they cast out devils; they shall speak with new tongues; They shall take up serpents; and if they drink any deadly thing, it shall not hurt them; they shall lay hands on the sick, and they shall recover. So~~

~~then after the Lord had spoken unto them,
he was received up into heaven, and sat on
the right hand of God. And they went forth,
and preached every where, the Lord work-
ing with~~ *~~them~~*~~, and confirming the word with
signs following. Amen~~.

These 12 verses take up a lot of room. So most Bibles place the words up in the text — but they write a disclaimer, saying something like "the most ancient manuscripts do not have this ending."

And somehow they separate verses 9-20 from the rest of the Bible text. They may also list one or two "alternate" endings as well (which are only found in a few perverted manuscripts).

Note: if the Bible you are checking is not listed below, it only means that these verses are not either omitted, italicized, bracketed or set apart.

It probably still has a footnote, declaring "most manuscripts," "the best manuscripts" or "the most ancient" do not have the verses.

Missing from: _ASV, _Bar, _CEV [223], [CSB], _ERV, [ESV], [GNB], (MOF) [224], *MRC*, [MSG], (NAB), *NAS*, *NAU*, [NCV], [NET], |NIrV [225], |NIV, _NLT,

---

223) The CEV labels these verses "One Old Ending to Mark's Gospel" and added the other (fake) ending as well, labeled "Another Old Ending to Mark's Gospel."
224) Moffatt (MOF) called verses 9-20 ending "(a)," but between verses 14-15 stuck in a totally different verse that came from Codex W. Then he added a second ending (b), with another verse someone added.
225) In "A Word about the NIrV," it says "Later copies of the Greek New Testament added several verses that the earlier ones don't have. Sometimes it's several verses in a row. When that's the case, we included them in the NIrV. But we set those verses off with a long line. That tells you that the first writers didn't write them. They were added later on." But if they don't believe they belong, why put them in their Bible? Because they still want you to buy their Bible.

[[NRS]], |NWT²²⁶, _Phi²²⁷, RSV, |TNIV, [WNT]

The following Bibles have Mark 16:9-20 in the text. But I have listed them separately with a raised F (ᶠ) because they also have a footnote that causes the reader to doubt that these 12 verses are truly scripture:

Missing from: AMPᶠ, BBEᶠ ²²⁸, CJBᶠ, GWNᶠ, ICBᶠ, ISVᶠ, JBᶠ, LBᶠ, NEBᶠ, NJBᶠ, REBᶠ

Luke 1:28 And the angel came in unto her, and said, Hail, *thou that art* highly favoured, the Lord is with thee: ~~blessed art thou among women~~.

Missing from: *AMP*²²⁹, ASV, Bar, BBE, CEV, CJB, CSB, *DBY*, ERV, ESV, GWN, ICB, ISV, JB, LB, MOF, NAB, NAS, NAU, NCV, NEB, NET, NIrV, NIV, NJB, NLT, NRS, NWT, Phi, REB, RSV, TNIV, WNT

Luke 8:43 And a woman having an issue of blood twelve years, which ~~had spent all her living upon physicians~~, neither could be healed of any,

Missing from: *AMP*, Bar, CJB, GWN, JB, MOF,

---

226) The NWT labels verses 9-20 the "Long Conclusion," writing this disclaimer: "Certain ancient manuscripts (A C D) and versions (Vg Syᶜˑᵖ) add the following long conclusion, but which א B Syˢ Arm omit."

227) Verses 9-20 appear in the JB Phillips (Phi) text, but they are set apart with this label: "*An Ancient Appendix.*" Clearly he did not believe these were the words of God (yet he put them in his Bible).

228) The BBE is way more subtle than most. It writes 16:8 as if it were broken off mid-sentence, ending the verse like this: "because they were full of fear that…" as if the original ending was lost. That's what many teach in Bible colleges today.

229) The AMP not only puts the words in italics; it actually goes far beyond God's words. In true Roman Catholic fashion, it falsely reads, "Blessed … are you *before* all other women." Mary wasn't a super-human goddess. She was just like other women, though blessed of God.

MRC, (NAB), NAS, NAU, NCV, NEB, NET, NIrV, NIV, NJB, NLT, NWT, Phi, REB, RSV, TNIV,

Luke 11:54 Laying wait for him, and seeking to catch something out of his mouth, ~~that they might accuse him~~.

Missing from: [AMP], ASV, Bar, CEV, CJB, CSB, *DBY*, ERV, ESV, GNB, GWN, ICB, ISV, JB, MOF, MRC, MSG, NAB, NAS, NAU, NCV, NEB, NET, NIrV, NIV, NJB, NRS, NWT, Phi, REB, RSV, TCW, TNIV, WNT

Luke 22:43 ~~And there appeared an angel unto him from heaven, strengthening him~~.

Look at how few versions were willing to stoop to remove these words in this and the next verse, from a critical time in the life of our Lord. Don't believe anyone who tries to tell you that textual criticism is a "science."

Missing from: [CSB], (NAB), Phi, RSV

Luke 22:44 ~~And being in an agony he prayed more earnestly: and his sweat was as it were great drops of blood falling down to the ground~~.

Missing from: [CSB], (NAB), Phi, RSV

Luke 23:17 ~~(For of necessity he must release one unto them at the feast.)~~

Missing from: *AMP*, *ASV*, Bar, BBE, CEV, CJB, [CSB], ERV, ESV, GNB, GWN, ICB, JB, LB, MOF, *MRC*, MSG, NAB, [NAS], [NAU], NCV, NEB,

NET, NIrV, NIV, NJB, NLT, NRS, NWT, Phi, REB, RSV, TNIV, WNT

Luke 23:23 And they were instant with loud voices, requiring that he might be crucified. And the voices of them ~~and of the chief priests~~ prevailed.

Missing from: AMP, ASV, Bar, BBE, CEV, CJB, CSB, *DBY*, DRA, ERV, ESV, GNB, GWN, ICB, ISV, JB, LB, MOF, MRC, MSG, NAB, NAS, NAU, NCV, NEB, NET, NIrV, NIV, NJB, NLT, NRS, NWT, Phi, REB, RSV, TNIV, WNT

Luke 23:38 And a superscription also was written over him ~~in letters of Greek, and Latin, and Hebrew~~, THIS IS THE KING OF THE JEWS.

Missing from: *AMP*, ASV, Bar, BBE, CEV, CJB, CSB, ERV, ESV, GNB, GWN, ICB, JB, LB, MRC, MSG, NAB, NAS, NAU, NCV, NEB, NET, NIrV, NIV, NJB, NLT, NRS, NWT, Phi, REB, RSV, TNIV, WNT

Luke 24:1 Now upon the first day of the week, very early in the morning, they came unto the sepulchre, bringing the spices which they had prepared, ~~and certain *others* with them~~.

Missing from: AMP, ASV, Bar, BBE, CEV, CJB, CSB, DBY, DRA, ERV, ESV, GNB, GWN, ICB, ISV, JB, LB, MOF, MRC, MSG, NAB, NAS, NAU, NCV, NEB, NET, NIrV, NIV, NJB, NLT, NRS, NWT, Phi, REB, RSV, TCW, TNIV, WNT

Luke 24:6 ~~He is not here, but is risen~~: remember how he spake unto you when he was yet in Galilee,

Missing from: NEB, [[NWT]], REB, RSV

Luke 24:12 ~~Then arose Peter, and ran unto the sepulchre; and stooping down, he beheld the linen clothes laid by themselves, and departed, wondering in himself at that which was come to pass~~.

Missing from: *MRC, NAS*, NEB, [[NWT]], REB, RSV

Luke 24:40 ~~And when he had thus spoken, he shewed them his hands and his feet.~~

Missing from: Bar, *MRC*, [NAS], NEB, [[NWT]], Phi, REB, RSV

Luke 24:42 And they gave him a piece of a broiled fish, ~~and of an honeycomb~~.

Missing from: AMP, ASV, Bar, ASV, BBE, CEV, CJB, CSB, ERV, ESV, GNB, GWN, ICB, ISV, JB, LB, MRC, MSG, NAB, NAS, NAU, NCV, NEB, NET, NIrV, NIV, NJB, NLT, NRS, NWT, Phi, REB, RSV, TCW, TNIV, WNT

Luke 24:51 And it came to pass, while he blessed them, he was parted from them, ~~and carried up into heaven~~.

Who would be foolish enough to remove these words? Acts 1:1-2 directly refers to them being here. After Gail

Riplinger made this obvious point in her *New Age Bible Versions*, the 1995 New American Standard Update had to put the words back into the text.

Missing from: MRC, NAS, NEB, REB

John 1:27 He it is, who coming after me ~~is preferred before me~~, whose shoe's latchet I am not worthy to unloose.

Missing from: ASV, Bar, BBE, CEV, CJB, CSB, DBY, ERV, ESV, GNB, GWN, ICB, ISV, JB, LB, MOF, MRC, NAB, NAS, NAU, NCV, NEB, NET, NIrV, NIV, NJB, NLT, NRS, NWT, Phi, REB, RSV, TNIV, WNT

If we remove these words, does John 5:1-15 make sense?

John 5:3 In these lay a great multitude of impotent folk, of blind, halt, withered, ~~waiting for the moving of the water~~.

Missing from: *AMP*, Bar, ASV, BBE, CEV, CJB, [CSB], *DBY*, ERV, ESV, GNB, GWN, ICB, (LB), [MOF], *MRC*, MSG, NAB, [NAS], [NAU], NCV, NEB, NET, NIrV, NIV, NJB, NLT, NRS, NWT, (Phi), REB, RSV, TNIV, WNT

John 5:4 ~~For an angel went down at a certain season into the pool, and troubled the water: whosoever then first after the troubling of the water stepped in was made whole of whatsoever disease he had~~.

Missing from: *AMP*, Bar, ASV, BBE, CEV, CJB, [CSB], *DBY*, ERV, ESV, GNB, GWN, ICB, (LB), [MOF], MSG, NAB, [NAS], [NAU], NCV, NEB,

NET, NIrV, NIV, NJB, NLT, NRS, NWT, (Phi), REB, RSV, TNIV, WNT

৩০   ৩০   ৩০

John 5:16 And therefore did the Jews perse-cute Jesus, ~~and sought to slay him~~, because he had done these things on the sabbath day.

Verse 18 says they "sought *the more* to kill him." They could only seek "the more" to kill him if they already sought to kill him previously.

Missing from: *AMP*, ASV, Bar, BBE, CEV, CJB, CSB, *DBY*, DRA, ERV, ESV, GNB, GWN, ICB, ISV, JB, LB, MOF, MRC, MSG, NAB, NAS, NAU, NCV, NEB, NET, NIrV, NIV, NJB, NLT, NRS, NWT, Phi, REB, RSV, TNIV, WNT

৩০   ৩০   ৩০

John 7:53-8:11 ~~And every man went unto his own house. Jesus went unto the mount of Olives. And early in the morning he came again into the temple, and all the people came unto him; and he sat down, and taught them. And the scribes and Pharisees brought unto him a woman taken in adultery; and when they had set her in the midst, They say unto him, Master, this woman was taken in adultery, in the very act. Now Moses in the law commanded us, that such should be stoned: but what sayest thou? This they said, tempting him, that they might have to ac-cuse him. But Jesus stooped down, and with *his* finger wrote on the ground, *as though he heard them not.* So when they continued ask-ing him, he lifted up himself, and said unto~~

~~them, He that is without sin among you, let him first cast a stone at her. And again he stooped down, and wrote on the ground. And they which heard *it*, being convicted by *their own* conscience, went out one by one, beginning at the eldest, *even* unto the last: and Jesus was left alone, and the woman standing in the midst. When Jesus had lifted up himself, and saw none but the woman, he said unto her, Woman, where are those thine accusers? hath no man condemned thee? She said, No man, Lord. And Jesus said unto her, Neither do I condemn thee: go, and sin no more.~~

Missing from: [ASV], *BBE*, [CSB], [ERV], [[ESV]], [GNB], [MOF], *MRC*, [NAS], [NAU], |NCV, NEB²³⁰, [NET], |NIrV, |NIV, _NLT, [[NRS]], |NWT, REB, RSV, |TNIV, [WNT]

The following Bibles have John 7:53-8:11 in the text. But I have listed them separately with a double raised-F (ᶠᶠ) because they also have a footnote that causes the reader to doubt that these 12 verses are truly scripture:

Missing from: AMP ᶠᶠ, Bar ᶠᶠ, Phi ᶠᶠ, CEV ᶠᶠ, CJB ᶠᶠ, GWN ᶠᶠ, ICB ᶠᶠ, ISV ᶠᶠ, JB ᶠᶠ, LB ᶠᶠ, NJB ᶠᶠ

❧   ❧   ❧

John 8:59 Then took they up stones to cast at him: but Jesus hid himself, and went out of the temple, ~~going through the midst of them, and so passed by.~~

---

230) The NEB and REB print this at the end of John, in a separate section, with a note both at 7:53 and the end of John, saying it "has no fixed place" in the gospel.

Missing from: AMP, ASV, Bar, BBE, CEV, CJB, CSB,
DBY, DRA, ERV, ESV, GNB, GWN, ICB, ISV, JB,
LB, MOF, MRC, MSG, NAB, NAS, NAU, NCV,
NEB, NET, NIrV, NIV, NJB, NLT, NRS, NWT, Phi,
REB, RSV, TNIV, WNT

WHAT'S MISSING?
DETAILS OF THE EARLY CHURCH

Acts 15:34 ~~Notwithstanding it pleased Silas
to abide there still~~.

Missing from: *AMP*, *ASV*, Bar, BBE, CEV, CJB,
CSB, DBY, ERV, ESV, GNB, GWN, ICB, *ISV*, JB,
LB, MOF, *MRC*, MSG, NAB, [NAS], [NAU], NCV,
NEB, NET, NIrV, NIV, NJB, NLT, NRS, NWT, Phi,
REB, RSV, TNIV, WNT

૭૦   ૭૦   ૭૦

Acts 24:6-8 records important details of the speech of
Tertullus. We see how he is twisting the facts to make it
look bad for Paul.

Acts 24:6 Who also hath gone about to pro-
fane the temple: whom we took, ~~and would
have judged according to our law~~.

Missing from: *AMP*, *ASV*, Bar, BBE, CEV, CJB,
[CSB], *DBY*, ERV, ESV, GNB, GWN, HNV, ICB,
ISV, MOF, *MRC*, MSG, NAB, [NAS], [NAU], NCV,
NEB, NIrV, NIV, NJB, NLT, NRS, NWT, Phi, REB,
RSV, TNIV, WEB, WNT

૭૦   ૭૦   ૭૦

Acts 24:7 ~~But the chief captain Lysias came
upon us, and with great violence took *him*
away out of our hands~~,

Missing from: *AMP*, *ASV*, Bar, BBE, CEV, CJB,
[CSB], *DBY*, ERV, ESV, GNB, GWN, HNV, ICB,
ISV, MOF, *MRC*, MSG, NAB, [NAS], [NAU], NCV,

NEB, NIrV, NIV, NJB, NLT, NRS, NWT, Phi, REB, RSV, TNIV, WNT

ცუ   ცუ   ცუ

Acts 24:8 ~~Commanding his accusers to come unto thee~~: by examining of whom thyself mayest take knowledge of all these things, whereof we accuse him.

Missing from: *AMP*, *ASV*, Bar, BBE, CEV, CJB, [CSB], *DBY*, ERV, ESV, GNB, GWN, HNV, ICB, ISV, MOF, *MRC*, MSG, NAB, [NAS], [NAU], NCV, NEB, NIrV, NIV, NJB, NLT, NRS, NWT, Phi, REB, RSV, TNIV, WNT

ცუ   ცუ   ცუ

Acts 28:16 And when we came to Rome, ~~the centurion delivered the prisoners to the captain of the guard: but~~ Paul was suffered to dwell by himself with a soldier that kept him.

Missing from: *AMP*, ASV, Bar, BBE, CEV, CJB, CSB, *DBY*, DRA, ERV, ESV, GNB, GWN, ICB, ISV, JB, LB, MOF, MRC, MSG, NAB, NAS, NAU, NCV, NEB, NET, NIrV, NIV, NJB, NLT, NRS, NWT, Phi, REB, RSV, TNIV, WNT

ცუ   ცუ   ცუ

Acts 28:29 ~~And when he had said these words, the Jews departed, and had great reasoning among themselves.~~

Missing from: *AMP*, *ASV*, Bar, BBE, CEV, CJB, [CSB], *DBY*, ERV, ESV, GNB, GWN, ICB, *ISV*, JB, LB, MOF, *MRC*, MSG, NAB, [NAS], [NAU], NCV, NEB, NET, NIrV, NIV, NJB, NLT, NRS, NWT, Phi, REB, RSV, TNIV, WNT

ცუ   ცუ   ცუ

MISSING DOCTRINES OF THE APOSTLES

What's Missing? Adultery

Galatians 5:19 Now the works of the flesh are manifest, which are *these*; ~~Adultery~~, fornication, uncleanness, lasciviousness,

Missing from: AMP, ASV, Bar, BBE, CEV, CJB, CSB, DBY, DRA[231], ERV, ESV, GNB, GWN, ICB, ISV, JB, LB, MOF, MRC, MSG, NAB, NAS, NAU, NCV[232], NEB, NET, NIrV, NIV, NJB, NLT, NRS, NWT, Phi, REB, RSV, TCW, TNIV, WNT

✤   ✤   ✤

James 4:4 Ye ~~adulterers and~~ adulteresses, know ye not that the friendship of the world is enmity with God? whosoever therefore will be a friend of the world is the enemy of God.

Why would the Alexandrians limit this sin to women?

Missing from: AMP, ASV, CJB, CSB, DBY, ERV, JB, LB, MRC, NAS, NAU, NWT, Phi, WNT

The following translations put some variation of "adulterous people," but hide that both genders are specified separately in the Greek text.

Missing from: Bar, BBE, CEV, DRA[233], ESV, GNB, GWN, ICB, ISV, MOF, MSG, NAB, NCV, NEB, NET, NIrV, NIV, NJB, NLT, NRS, REB, RSV, TCW, TNIV

---

231) The Catholic DRA removes "adultery" but adds "luxury."
232) The NCV seems to do the opposite: it translates *adultery* as "being sexually unfaithful," but then removes *fornication*, which is *any* sex outside of marriage — even though every manuscript has it.
233) The DRA, ISV, NAB, NET, NJB, NLT and NRS have "adulterers," but remove "adulteresses," which is in *every* Greek manuscript.

What's Missing? Fornication

> Romans 1:29 Being filled with all unrigh-
> teousness, ~~fornication~~, wickedness, covetous-
> ness, maliciousness; full of envy, murder, de-
> bate, deceit, malignity; whisperers,

Fornication is an important sin. That is why 1/4 of Americans have at least one of 25 STDs. Can you trust a Bible that removes "fornication" from this list of sins?

Missing from: AMP, ASV, Bar, BBE, CEV, CJB, CSB, DBY, DRA, ERV, ESV, GNB, GWN[234], ICB, ISV, JB, LB, MOF, MRC, MSG, NAB, NAS, NAU, NCV, NEB, NET, NIrV, NIV, NJB, NLT, NRS, NWT ,Phi, REB, RSV, TNIV, WNT

What's Missing? Other Words God Wrote Through the Apostles and Early Church Leaders

> Acts 15:18 Known ~~unto God are all his works~~ from the beginning of the world.

Missing from: AMP, ASV, Bar, BBE, CEV, CJB, CSB, DBY, ERV, ESV, GNB, GWN, ICB, ISV, JB, LB, MOF, MRC, MSG, NAB, NAS, NAU, NCV, NEB, NET, NIrV, NIV, NJB, NLT, NRS, NWT, Phi, REB, RSV, TCW, TNIV, WNT

> Romans 9:32 Wherefore? Because *they sought it* not by faith, but as it were by the

---

234) GWN removes both "unrighteousness" and "fornication" and inserts "all kinds of sexual sins."

works ~~of the law~~. For they stumbled at that stumblingstone;

This is about the Law of Moses, not "anything a person does," as many translations read.

Missing from: AMP, ASV, Bar, BBE, CJB, CSB, DBY, DRA, ERV, ESV, GNB, GWN, ICB, ISV, JB, MOF, MRC, MSG, NAB, NAS, NAU, NCV, NEB, NET, NIrV, NIV, NJB, NRS, NWT, Phi, REB, RSV, TCW[235], TNIV, WNT

୨ଡ଼   ୨ଡ଼   ୨ଡ଼

Romans 14:6 He that regardeth the day, regardeth *it* unto the Lord; ~~and he that regardeth not the day, to the Lord he doth not regard it.~~ He that eateth, eateth to the Lord, for he giveth God thanks; and he that eateth not, to the Lord he eateth not, and giveth God thanks.

Missing from: AMP, ASV, Bar, BBE, CEV, CJB, CSB, DBY, DRA, ERV, ESV, GNB, GWN, ICB, ISV, JB, LB, MOF, MRC, MSG, NAB, NAS, NAU, NCV, NEB, NIrV, NIV, NJB, NLT, NRS, Phi, REB, RSV, TCW[236], TNIV, WNT

୨ଡ଼   ୨ଡ଼   ୨ଡ଼

Romans 14:21 *It is* good neither to eat flesh, nor to drink wine, nor *any thing* whereby thy brother stumbleth, ~~or is offended, or is made weak~~.

---

235) Amazingly, TCW removes the entire sentence, "Because they sought it not by faith, but as it were by the works of the law," which shows that faith is the answer, not legalism.

236) TCW is missing not just the lined-out words, but the whole first sentence, which says it is between a person and the Lord whether he regards one day above another or not.

Missing from: ASV, Bar, BBE, CJB, CSB, ERV, ESV, GNB, GWN, ICB, LB, MOF, MSG, NAB, NAS, NAU, NCV, NEB, NET, NIrV, NIV, NLT, NRS, NWT, Phi, REB, RSV, TCW, TNIV, WNT

❧   ❧   ❧

1 Corinthians 7:39 The wife is bound ~~by the law~~ as long as her husband liveth; but if her husband be dead, she is at liberty to be married to whom she will; only in the Lord.

Missing from: ASV, Bar, BBE, CEV, CJB, CSB, DBY, ERV, ESV, GNB, GWN, ICB, ISV, JB, LB, MOF, MRC, MSG, NAB, NAS, NAU, NCV, NEB, NET, NIrV, NIV, NJB, NLT, NRS, NWT, Phi, REB, RSV, TNIV, WNT

❧   ❧   ❧

1 Corinthians 10:28 But if any man say unto you, This is offered in sacrifice unto idols, eat not for his sake that shewed it, and for conscience sake: ~~for the earth is the Lord's, and the fulness thereof~~:

Missing from: AMP, ASV, Bar, BBE, CEV, CJB, CSB, DBY, DRA, ERV, ESV, GNB, GWN, ICB, ISV, JB, LB, MOF, MRC, MSG, NAB, NAS, NAU, NCV, NEB, NET, NIrV, NIV, NLT, NRS, NWT, Phi, REB, RSV, TCW, TNIV, WNT

❧   ❧   ❧

1 Corinthians 11:24 And when he had given thanks, he brake *it*, and said, ~~Take, eat:~~ this is my body, which is ~~broken~~ for you: this do in remembrance of me.

The bread was broken because it was a symbol of Jesus' body being "broken" for them. Removing these words removes this doctrinal understanding.

Missing from: *AMP*[237], ASV, Bar, BBE, CEV[238], CJB, CSB, DBY, DRA[239], ERV, ESV, GNB, GWN, ICB, ISV, JB, LB, MOF[240], MRC, MSG, NAB, NAS, NAU, NCV, NEB, NET, NIrV, NIV, NJB, NLT, NRS, NWT, Phi, REB, RSV, TNIV, WNT

1 Corinthians 11:29 For he that eateth and drinketh ~~unworthily~~, eateth and drinketh damnation to himself, not discerning the Lord's body.

Missing from: AMP, ASV, Bar, BBE, CEV, CJB, CSB, DBY, ERV, ESV, GNB, GWN, ICB, ISV, JB, MOF, MRC, MSG, NAB, NAS, NAU, NCV, NEB, NET, NIrV, NIV, NJB, NLT, NRS, NWT, REB, RSV, TNIV, WNT

Galatians 3:1 O foolish Galatians, who hath bewitched you, ~~that ye should not obey the truth~~, before whose eyes Jesus Christ hath been evidently set forth, crucified among you?

The Galatians weren't just bewitched; they stopped obeying the truth.

Missing from: AMP, ASV, Bar, BBE, CEV, CJB, CSB, DBY, ERV, ESV, GNB, GWN ,ICB, ISV, JB, LB, MOF, MRC, MSG, NAB, NAS, NAU, NCV, NEB, NET ,NIrV, NIV, NJB, NLT, NRS, NWT, Phi, REB, RSV, TNIV, WNT

---

237) The AMP italicizes "Take, eat," but keeps "broken."
238) The CEV and NLT remove "Take, eat" but replace "broken" with "given."
239) The DRA keeps "Take, eat" but replaces "broken" with "shall be delivered."
240) MOF, MSG and WNT remove "Take, eat" but don't remove "broken."

Ephesians 5:30 For we are members of his body, ~~of his flesh, and of his bones~~.

This is the same mystery Paul wrote about two verses later: the church is like a wife to Christ. God has Paul say we are "bone of [Christ's] bones and flesh of [Christ's] flesh."

Without these words, Paul seems to ramble in the next two verses. With these words, the change of topic makes sense.

Missing from: AMP, ASV, Bar, BBE, CEV, CJB, CSB, *DBY*, ERV, ESV, GNB, GWN, ICB, JB, LB, MOF, MRC, MSG, NAB, NAS, NAU, NCV, NEB, NET ,NIrV, NIV, NJB, NLT, NRS, NWT, Phi, REB, RSV, TCW, TNIV, WNT

Philippians 3:16 Nevertheless, whereto we have already attained, let us walk by the same ~~rule, let us mind the same thing~~.

Missing from: AMP, ASV, Bar, BBE, CEV, CJB, CSB, DBY, ERV, ESV, GNB, GWN, ICB, ISV, JB, LB, MOF, MRC, MSG, NAB, NAS, NAU, NCV, NEB, NET, NIrV, NIV, NJB, NLT, NRS, NWT, Phi, REB, RSV, TNIV, WNT

Colossians 3:6 For which things' sake the wrath of God cometh ~~on the children of disobedience~~:

Missing from: Bar, ESV, ICB, JB, LB, MRC, MSG, (NAB), NAS, NCV, NEB, NIrV, NIV, NLT, NWT, REB, RSV, TCW, TNIV, WNT

1 Timothy 1:17 Now unto the King eternal,

immortal, invisible, the only ~~wise~~ God, *be* honour and glory for ever and ever. Amen.

Missing from: AMP, ASV, Bar, BBE, CEV, CJB, CSB, DBY, DRA, ERV, ESV, GNB, GWN, ICB, ISV, JB, MOF, MRC, MSG, NAB, NAS, NAU, NCV, NEB, NET, NIrV, NIV, NJB, NLT, NRS, NWT, Phi, REB, RSV, TCW, TNIV, WNT

1 Timothy 5:16 If any ~~man or~~ woman that believeth have widows, let them relieve them, and let not the church be charged; that it may relieve them that are widows indeed.

Missing from: *AMP*, ASV, BBE, CEV, CJB, CSB, ERV, ESV, GNB, GWN, ICB, ISV, JB, MRC, MSG, NAB, NAS, NAU, NET, NIrV, NIV, NJB, NLT, NRS, NWT, REB, RSV, TNIV, WNT

1 Timothy 6:5 Perverse disputings of men of corrupt minds, and destitute of the truth, supposing that gain is godliness: ~~from such withdraw thyself~~.

There are a lot of Christians who need to "withdraw themselves" from false teachers who tell them they must "get things" to be godly. But they stay and are deceived, because their Bibles don't have these words of warning.

Missing from: *AMP*, Bar, BBE, CEV, CJB, CSB, DBY, DRA, ERV, ESV, GNB, GWN, ICB, ISV, JB, MOF, MRC, MSG, NAB, NAS, NAU, NCV, NEB, NET, NIrV, NIV, NJB, NLT, NRS, NWT, Phi, REB, RSV, TCW, TNIV, WNT

2 Timothy 1:11 Whereunto I am appointed a

preacher, and an apostle, and a teacher ~~of the Gentiles~~.

Missing from: *AMP*, ASV, Bar, BBE, CEV, CSB, ERV, ESV, GNB, GWN, ICB, JB, MOF, MRC, MSG, NAB, NAS, NAU, NCV, NEB, NET, NIrV, NIV, NJB, NLT, NRS, NWT, Phi, REB, RSV, TNIV

Hebrews 3:6 But Christ as a son over his own house; whose house are we, if we hold fast the confidence and the rejoicing of the hope ~~firm unto the end~~.

Missing from: *AMP*, Bar, CEV, CJB, CSB, ESV, GNB, GWN, ICB, ISV, JB, MOF, MSG, NAB, NCV, NET, NIrV, NIV, NJB, NLT, NRS, REB, RSV, TCW, TNIV [241]

Hebrews 7:21 (For those priests were made without an oath; but this with an oath by him that said unto him, The Lord sware and will not repent, Thou art a priest for ever ~~after the order of Melchisedec~~:)

Missing from: *AMP*, ASV, Bar [242], BBE, CEV, CJB, CSB, *DBY*, DRA, ERV, ESV, GNB, GWN, ICB, ISV, JB, MOF, MRC, MSG, NAB, NAS, NAU, NCV, NET, NIrV, NIV, NJB, NLT, NRS, NWT, Phi, REB, RSV, TNIV, WNT

1 Peter 4:14 If ye be reproached for the name of Christ, happy *are ye*; for the spirit of glory

---

241) The TNIV and NRS chose to keep "firm," but are still missing "unto the end," unlike almost every Greek manuscript.
242) Barclay (Bar) is also missing "Thou art a priest forever," even though every Greek text has it.

and of God resteth upon you: ~~on their part he is evil spoken of, but on your part he is glorified~~.

Missing from: *AMP*, ASV, Bar, BBE, CEV, CJB, CSB, *DBY*, DRA, ERV, ESV, GNB, GWN, ICB, ISV, JB, LB, MOF, MRC, MSG, NAB, NAS, NAU, NCV, NEB, NET, NIrV, NIV, NJB, NLT, NRS, NWT, Phi, REB, RSV, TNIV, WNT

℘   ℘   ℘

1 Peter 5:5 Likewise, ye younger, submit yourselves unto the elder. Yea, all *of you* ~~be subject~~ one to another, and be clothed with humility: for God resisteth the proud, and giveth grace to the humble.

People can "have humility" toward each other and still not "be subject" to one another. Being *subject* to one another shows the "priesthood of all believers," rather than submitting to a priest who is over the others.

When you read the "modern" versions you'll need to read this verse very carefully to see what is missing. They covered it up in a tricky way.

Missing from: AMP, Bar, BBE[243], CEV, CJB, CSB, DBY, DRA, ESV, ICB, ISV, JB, MOF, MRC, MSG[244], NAB, NAS, NAU, NCV, NEB, NET, NIrV, NIV, NJB, NRS, NWT, REB, RSV, TCW, TNIV, WNT

℘   ℘   ℘

1 Peter 5:11 To him be ~~glory and~~ dominion for ever and ever. Amen.

Missing from: AMP, ASV, Bar, BBE, CEV, CJB, CSB,

---

243) The BBE gives the idea of being servants, but removes that it is "one to another."
244) The MSG changes the meaning entirely, to "be down to earth with each other."

ERV, ESV, GNB, GWN, ICB, ISV, JB, LB, MOF, MRC, MSG, NAB, NAS, NAU, NCV, NEB, NET, NIrV, NIV, NJB, NLT, NRS, NWT, Phi, REB, RSV, TNIV, WNT

༄ ༄ ༄

1 Peter 5:14 Greet ye one another with a kiss of charity. Peace *be* with you all that are in Christ ~~Jesus. Amen~~.

Missing from: *AMP*, ASV, Bar, BBE, CEV, CJB, CSB, DBY, ERV, ESV, GNB, GWN, ICB, ISV, JB, LB, MOF[245], MRC, MSG, NAB, NAS, NAU, NCV, NEB, NET, NIV, NJB, NLT, NRS, NWT, Phi, REB, RSV, TCW, TNIV, WNT

༄ ༄ ༄

2 Peter 1:21 For the prophecy came not in old time by the will of man: but ~~holy~~ men of God spake *as they were* moved by the Holy Ghost.

Missing from: AMP, ASV, Bar, BBE, CEV[246], CJB, CSB, ERV, ESV, GNB, GWN, ICB, ISV, JB, LB, MRC, MSG, NAB, NAS, NAU, NCV, NEB, NET, NIrV, NIV, NJB, NLT, NRS, NWT, Phi, REB, RSV, TNIV, WNT

༄ ༄ ༄

1 John 4:19 We love ~~him~~, because he first loved us.

We love *God* because He first loved us. This verse is not talking about loving just *anyone*.

Missing from: *AMP*, Bar, BBE, CEV, CJB, CSB, DBY, ERV, ESV, GNB, GWN, ICB, ISV, JB, MOF, MRC, MSG, NAB, NAS, NAU, NCV, NEB, NET,

---

245) Moffatt (MOF) kept "Jesus" but removed "Amen."
246) The CEV removes the entire phrase, "holy men of God."

NIrV, NIV, NJB, NLT[247], NRS, NWT, Phi, REB, RSV, TNIV, WNT

Jude 1:25 To the only ~~wise~~ God our Saviour, *be* glory and majesty, dominion and power, both now and ever. Amen.

Missing from: AMP, ASV, Bar, BBE, CEV[248], CJB, CSB, DBY, DRA, ERV, ESV, GNB, GWN, ICB, ISV, JB, LB, MOF, MRC, MSG, NAB, NAS, NAU, NCV, NEB, NET, NIrV, NIV, NJB, NLT, NRS, NWT, Phi, REB, RSV, TNIV, WNT

Revelation 11:15 And the seventh angel sounded; and there were great voices in heaven, saying, The kingdoms of this world ~~are~~ become ~~*the kingdoms*~~ of our Lord, and of his Christ; and he shall reign for ever and ever.

The plural "kingdoms" are changed to the singular "kingdom."

Missing from: AMP, ASV, Bar[249], BBE, CEV, CJB, CSB, DBY, DRA, ERV, ESV, GNB[250], GWN, HNV, ICB, ISV, JB, LB, MOF[251], MRC, MSG, NAB, NAS, NAU, NCV, NEB[252], NET, NIrV, NIV, NJB, NLT, NRS, NWT, Phi[253], REB, RSV, TNIV, WEB, WNT

---

247) The NLT not only removed "him" (God), but changed it to "We love *each other.*"
248) The CEV not only removes "wise" but also shoves the word "only" back to the previous verse.
249) Barclay (Bar) removes the entire section about "kingdoms."
250) The GNB and NCV substitute "power" for "kingdom(s)."
251) Moffatt (MOF) substitutes "reign" for "kingdom(s)."
252) The NEB and WNT substitute "sovereignty" for "kingdom(s)."
253) JB Phillips (Phi) substitutes "kingship" for "kingdom(s)."

Revelation 12:12 Therefore rejoice, *ye* heavens, and ye that dwell in them. Woe to ~~the inhabiters of~~ the earth and of the sea! for the devil is come down unto you, having great wrath, because he knoweth that he hath but a short time.

It is the *people*, not the planet, who are threatened by the devil coming down in his "great wrath."

Missing from: AMP, ASV, Bar, BBE, CEV, CJB, CSB, DBY, DRA, ERV, ESV, GNB, GWN, HNV, ICB, ISV, JB, MOF, MRC, MSG, NAB, NAS, NAU, NCV, NEB, NET, NIrV, NIV, NJB, NLT, NRS, NWT, Phi, RSV, TCW, TNIV, WEB, WNT

18

WHAT'S MISSING... AT A GLANCE

CHART A
ALPHABETICAL ORDER BY VERSION

Words, phrases and verses missing, italicized, bracketed, or otherwise set apart as "not belonging in the Bible." From the 257 sample verses listed in Chapter 17.

VERSION	MISSING	ITALICS	BRACKETS / SET APART	TOTAL (257 POSSIBLE)
AMP	82	112	7	201
ASV	177	16	24	217
Bar	216	0	12	228
BBE	196	12	0	208
CEV	202	0	12	214
CJB	209	0	0	209
CSB	188	0	46	234
DBY	149	46	0	195

VERSION	MISSING	ITALICS	BRACKETS / SET APART	TOTAL (257 POSSIBLE)
DRA	91	0	0	91
ERV	193	0	24	217
ESV	210	0	24	234
GNB	206	0	24	230
GWN	206	2	0	208
HNV	37	0	0	37
ICB	198	0	0	198
ISV	172	5	0	177
JB	206	0	0	206
LB	153	0	3	156
MOF	190	0	24	214
MRC	189	36	0	225
MSG	196	0	12	208
NAB	207	0	23	230
NAS	191	0	47	238
NAU	187	0	45	232
NCV	200	0	24	224
NEB	214	0	12	226
NET	210	0	24	234
NIrV	208	0	24	232
NIV	222	0	24	246
NJB	203	0	0	203
NLT	201	0	24	225
NRS	214	0	24	238
NWT	209	0	28	237
Phi	198	0	15	213
REB	220	0	0	220
RSV	245	0	0	245
TCW	94	0	0	94
TNIV	218	0	24	242
WEB	34	0	0	34
WNT	204	0	24	228

CHART B
IN ORDER OF THE NUMBER OF VERSES AFFECTED

VERSION	MISSING	ITALICS	BRACKETS / SET APART	VERSES AFFECTED (OUT OF 257)	% OF 257
NIV	222	0	24	246	95.72%
RSV	245	0	0	245	95.33%
TNIV	218	0	24	242	94.16%
NAS	191	0	47	238	92.61%
NRS	214	0	24	238	92.61%
NWT	209	0	28	237	92.22%
CSB	188	0	46	234	91.05%
ESV	210	0	24	234	91.05%
NET	210	0	24	234	91.05%
NIrV	208	0	24	232	90.27%
NAU	187	0	45	232	90.27%
NAB	207	0	23	230	89.49%
GNB	206	0	24	230	89.49%
WNT	204	0	24	228	88.72%
Bar	216	0	12	228	88.72%
NEB	214	0	12	226	87.94%
MRC	189	36	0	225	87.55%
NLT	201	0	24	225	87.55%
NCV	200	0	24	224	87.16%
REB	220	0	0	220	85.60%
ERV	193	0	24	217	84.44%
ASV	177	16	24	217	84.44%
MOF	190	0	24	214	83.27%
CEV	202	0	12	214	83.27%
Phi	198	0	15	213	82.88%
CJB	209	0	0	209	81.32%
BBE	196	12	0	208	80.93%
GWN	206	2	0	208	80.93%
MSG	196	0	12	208	80.93%
JB	206	0	0	206	80.16%

VERSION	MISSING	ITALICS	BRACKETS / SET APART	VERSES AFFECTED (OUT OF 257)	% OF 257
NJB	203	0	0	203	78.99%
AMP	82	112	7	201	78.21%
ICB	198	0	0	198	77.04%
DBY	149	46	0	195	75.88%
ISV	172	5	0	177	68.87%
LB	153	0	3	156	60.70%
TCW	94	0	0	94	36.58%
DRA	91	0	0	91	35.41%
HNV	37	0	0	37	14.40%
WEB	34	0	0	34	13.23%

CHART C
IN ORDER OF DATE OF PUBLICATION

VERSION	MISSING	ITALICS	BRACKETS/ SET APART	#/257	%/257	YEAR
ERV	193	0	24	217	84.44%	1881
DBY	149	46	0	195	75.88%	1884
DRA	91	0	0	91	35.41%	1899
ASV	177	16	24	217	84.44%	1901
WNT	204	0	24	228	88.72%	1912
RSV	245	0	0	245	95.33%	1946
BBE	196	12	0	208	80.93%	1949
MOF	190	0	24	214	83.27%	1950
AMP	82	112	7	201	78.21%	1954
Phi	198	0	15	213	82.88%	1958
NEB	214	0	12	226	87.94%	1961
JB	206	0	0	206	80.16%	1967
Bar	216	0	12	228	88.72%	1968
NAB	207	0	23	230	89.49%	1970
LB	153	0	3	156	60.70%	1971

VERSION	MISSING	ITALICS	BRACKETS/ SET APART	#/257	%/257	YEAR
NIV	222	0	24	246	95.72%	1978
NAS	191	0	47	238	92.61%	1977
NJB	203	0	0	203	78.99%	1985
ICB	198	0	0	198	77.04%	1986
NCV	200	0	24	224	87.16%	1987
NRS	214	0	24	238	92.61%	1989
REB	220	0	0	220	85.60%	1989
GNB	206	0	24	230	89.49%	1992
NAU	187	0	45	232	90.27%	1995
NIrV	208	0	24	232	90.27%	1995
GWN	206	2	0	208	80.93%	1995
CEV	202	0	12	214	83.27%	1995
CJB	209	0	0	209	81.32%	1998
TNIV	218	0	24	242	94.16%	2001
CSB	188	0	46	234	91.05%	2001
ESV	210	0	24	234	91.05%	2001
MSG	196	0	12	208	80.93%	2002
MRC	189	36	0	225	87.55%	2003
TCW	94	0	0	94	36.58%	2003
NET	210	0	24	234	91.05%	2004
NLT	201	0	24	225	87.55%	2004
NWT	209	0	28	237	92.22%	2006
ISV	172	5	0	177	68.87%	2009[1]
HNV	37	0	0	37	14.40%	2009[2]
WEB	34	0	0	34	13.23%	2009[3]

1) As of 2009, the International Standard Version is almost complete.
2) As of 2009, the Hebrew Names Version (based on the WEB) is a translation in progress.
3) As of 2009, the World English Bible is a translation in progress.

AFTERWORD

When you read a book, you encounter its author. Or authors. When you read a Bible, but with words added to it and taken away from it, all you find out is men's opinions.

You do not find out what God said.

We have seen what the King James Bible says, and weighed it against 40 different Bible versions. Every one of them was missing words, phrases and verses that God put into the Bible.

None of them could even agree as to what words should be taken away. Every one of those Bible versions was man's opinions about what they think God *should* have said.

Not one of them can be considered God's words.

But when you read God's words, as He wanted you to have them, with nothing added and nothing taken away, you are not reading a book like any other book in the world.

You are reading *The Book*. And you come face to face with the Person behind it.

The purpose of this book is to show you how important

it is to get beyond man's opinions, to God's holy words, and to God Himself, who stands behind His words.

Pray to God and ask Him, and He will help you understand His Bible.

May God bless you, as He has blessed me, as you read His preserved words in English, the King James Bible. And may His Spirit give you understanding in all these things.

In Christ Jesus, and for His service,

David W. Daniels

Index of Scriptures

Genesis 3:1 53
Genesis 3:1-5 58
Numbers 23:19 21
Deuteronomy 4:2 3, 32
Deuteronomy 12:32 3
Deuteronomy 29:29 84
Psalm 12:6-7 45, 51, 63, 84
Psalm 118:8-9 99
Proverbs 30:5-6 3
Isaiah 7:14 76
Isaiah 40:8 84
Matthew 1:25 90, 97, 180
Matthew 5:18 84
Matthew 5:22 131, 197
Matthew 5:44 131, 206
Matthew 6:13 206
Matthew 6:33 172
Matthew 8:29 153
Matthew 9:13 98, 131, 189, 190
Matthew 12:35 131, 206
Matthew 12:47 70, 214
Matthew 13:51 122, 147
Matthew 13:58 50
Matthew 15:6 131, 206-207
Matthew 15:8 131, 207
Matthew 16:2b-3 47-49, 138, 207

Matthew 16:3 131, 207
Matthew 16:20 122, 131, 153
Matthew 17:21 87, 130, 138, 204, 205
Matthew 17:22 96, 101, 153
Matthew 18:2 154
Matthew 18:11 130, 138, 190
Matthew 19:9 131, 208
Matthew 19:16 182, 183
Matthew 19:17 131, 172, 183
Matthew 20:7 131, 208
Matthew 20:16 131, 193
Matthew 20:22 131, 190
Matthew 21:44 75, 130, 138, 197
Matthew 22:30 131, 201
Matthew 23:8 122, 131, 157
Matthew 23:14 75, 130, 138, 197
Matthew 24:7 131, 208
Matthew 24:35 42, 51, 63, 84
Matthew 25:13 131, 195-196
Matthew 25:31 131, 201
Matthew 26:28 131, 188
Matthew 27:24 215
Matthew 28:6 122, 148

Mark 1:1 121-122, 180
Mark 1:14 215
Mark 1:42 215
Mark 2:17 131, 190, 194
Mark 3:15 191
Mark 4:11 131, 209
Mark 6:11 75, 131, 198
Mark 7:16 138, 209
Mark 8:26 131, 209
Mark 9:24 122, 148
Mark 9:29 87, 204
Mark 9:42 210
Mark 9:44 75, 88, 130, 138, 194
Mark 9:45 75, 88, 195
Mark 9:46 75, 88, 130, 138, 195
Mark 9:49 131, 210
Mark 10:21 131, 191
Mark 10:24 131, 188
Mark 11:10 216
Mark 11:26 130, 138, 210
Mark 12:23 196
Mark 12:30 131, 211
Mark 13:14 131, 211
Mark 13:31 42, 51, 63, 84
Mark 13:33 131, 203
Mark 14:18 96, 101, 154
Mark 14:24 131, 188
Mark 14:68 90, 216
Mark 15:28 98, 130, 138, 216
Mark 16:9-20 76, 130, 138-140, 217-219
Luke 1:28 219
Luke 2:40 184
Luke 4:4 131, 157, 172
Luke 4:8 87, 131, 203
Luke 4:18 131, 192
Luke 4:21 44
Luke 4:41 122
Luke 8:43 219
Luke 9:26 34

Luke 9:54 192
Luke 9:55 192-193
Luke 9:55b-56 36-37, 41, 131
Luke 9:56 193
Luke 9:57 122, 148
Luke 11:2 131, 176
Luke 11:4 131, 176
Luke 11:11 131, 211
Luke 11:29 131, 212
Luke 11:54 220
Luke 12:2 38
Luke 17:6 96, 149
Luke 20:23 131, 212
Luke 21:4 131, 173
Luke 22:31 122, 149
Luke 21:33 42, 51, 63, 84
Luke 22:43 142, 201 220
Luke 22:43-44 70, 130
Luke 22:44 142, 220
Luke 22:68 131, 212
Luke 23:17 130, 142, 220
Luke 23:23 221
Luke 23:38 221
Luke 23:42 122, 149
Luke 24:1 221
Luke 24:6 70, 222
Luke 24:12 70, 143, 222
Luke 24:36 90, 213
Luke 24:40 70, 90, 143, 222
Luke 24:42 222
Luke 24:51 88, 90, 222
John 1:14 177
John 1:18 97, 110, 178
John 1:27 223
John 3:5 114-115
John 3:13 131, 199
John 3:15 131, 213
John 3:16 115, 131, 179
John 3:18 131, 179
John 4:42 122, 157

John 5:3 223
John 5:4 130, 143, 202, 223
John 5:16 224
John 5:18 224
John 6:47 98, 131, 185
John 7:8 27, 41, 213
John 7:8-9 24
John 7:53-8:11 76, 130, 143-145, 224-225
John 8:59 225
John 16:10 131, 176
John 16:16 131, 177
John 17:12 131, 199
Acts 1:21 107
Acts 2:30 122, 158
Acts 3:26 122, 154
Acts 7:30 202
Acts 8:37 31-33, 41, 65, 98, 130, 145, 185
Acts 10:30 87, 204
Acts 15:11 122, 158
Acts 15:18 229
Acts 15:34 122, 145, 226
Acts 16:31 122, 159, 185
Acts 19:4 122, 159
Acts 20:21 122, 159
Acts 20:25 173
Acts 23:9 173
Acts 24:6 226
Acts 24:7 130, 145, 226
Acts 24:8 227
Acts 24:15 196
Acts 28:16 227
Acts 28:29 130, 146, 227
Romans 1:16 122, 159-160
Romans 1:27 117
Romans 1:29 229
Romans 6:11 122, 150
Romans 8:1 183
Romans 9:32 229-230

Romans 10:4 108-109
Romans 10:15 193
Romans 11:6 189
Romans 14:6 230
Romans 14:21 230
Romans 15:8 122, 155
Romans 15:29 194
Romans 16:20 122, 160
Romans 16:24 122, 130, 146, 169
1 Corinthians 5:4 122, 160
1 Corinthians 5:5 78, 122, 155
1 Corinthians 5:7 186
1 Corinthians 6:20 184
1 Corinthians 7:5 87, 204-205
1 Corinthians 7:39 231
1 Corinthians 9:1 122, 161
1 Corinthians 9:18 96, 122, 161
1 Corinthians 10:28 231
1 Corinthians 11:24 231
1 Corinthians 11:29 232
1 Corinthians 15:21 99
1 Corinthians 15:47 122, 150
1 Corinthians 16:22 122, 168
1 Corinthians 16:23 122, 162
2 Corinthians 4:6 122, 155
2 Corinthians 4:10 122, 151
2 Corinthians 5:18 122, 156
2 Corinthians 11:31 122, 162
Galatians 3:1 232
Galatians 3:17 122, 162
Galatians 4:7 122, 163
Galatians 5:19 228
Galatians 6:15 122, 168
Galatians 6:17 122, 161
Ephesians 3:9 122, 168
Ephesians 3:14 122, 169
Ephesians 5:30 233
Philippians 3:16 233
Philippians 4:13 122, 163

Colossians 1:2 122, 170
Colossians 1:14 187
Colossians 1:28 122, 156
Colossians 2:18 202-203
Colossians 3:6 78, 91, 233
1 Thessalonians 2:19 122, 163
1 Thessalonians 3:11 122, 164
1 Thessalonians 3:13 122, 164
2 Thessalonians 1:8 122, 164
2 Thessalonians 1:12 122, 165
1 Timothy 1:1 122, 161
1 Timothy 1:9-10 118
1 Timothy 1:17 233-234
1 Timothy 2:7 122, 165
1 Timothy 3:16 64, 174
1 Timothy 4:12 184
1 Timothy 5:16 234
1 Timothy 5:21 122, 151-152
1 Timothy 6:5 234
2 Timothy 1:11 234-235
2 Timothy 3:15 43
2 Timothy 3:16 65
2 Timothy 3:16-17 43
2 Timothy 4:1 152
2 Timothy 4:22 122, 169
Titus 1:4 122, 152
Hebrews 1:3 187
Hebrews 3:1 122, 165
Hebrews 3:6 235
Hebrews 7:21 235
Hebrews 10:34 200
James 4:4 228
1 Peter 1:22 183
1 Peter 1:23-25 84
1 Peter 4:1 186
1 Peter 4:14 235-236
1 Peter 5:5 236
1 Peter 5:10 122, 156
1 Peter 5:11 236
1 Peter 5:14 237

2 Peter 1:16 55
2 Peter 1:21 237
1 John 1:1-3 55-56
1 John 1:7 122, 166
1 John 4:3 122, 166
1 John 4:9 180
1 John 4:19 237
1 John 5:7 62, 64
1 John 5:7-8 122, 171
1 John 5:8 171
1 John 5:13 174
2 John 1:3 122, 153
2 John 1:9-11 133
Jude 1:25 238
Revelation 1:8 97, 131, 181
Revelation 1:9 122, 167
Revelation 1:11 97, 131, 181
Revelation 2:15 131, 214
Revelation 5:14 181
Revelation 11:15 238
Revelation 11:17 98, 182
Revelation 12:12 239
Revelation 12:17 122, 167
Revelation 14:5 175
Revelation 16:17 200
Revelation 20:9 175
Revelation 22:18-19 3, 33, 63
Revelation 22:21 122, 167

INDEX BY BIBLE VERSION

AMP = Amplified Bible
15, 39-41, 49, 108-113, 138-140, 142-143, 145-177, 179-217, 219-239, 240, 243

ASV = American Standard Version
15, 16, 17, 27, 37, 41, 49, 58, 62, 66-67, 69, 70, 72, 83, 85, 104, 106-107, 121, 129, 138-177, 180-198, 200-239, 240, 242, 243

Bar = The New Testament: A New Translation
15, 33, 37, 49, 138-143, 145-187, 189-239, 240, 242, 243

BBE = Bible in Basic English
15, 33, 37, 49, 121, 138-140, 142-184, 186-217, 219-239, 240, 242, 243

CEV = Contemporary English Version
15, 27, 33, 37, 49, 138-143, 145-184, 186-239, 240, 242, 244

CJB = Complete Jewish Bible
15, 33, 37, 49, 138-140, 142-143, 145-206, 208-217, 219-239, 240, 242, 244

CSB = Holman Christian Standard Bible
15, 37, 41, 49, 124-132, 138-239, 240, 242, 244

DBY = Darby Bible
15, 27, 33, 41, 49, 139-140, 143, 145-148, 150-153, 155-165, 167-177, 181-198, 200—214, 216-217, 219-221, 223-224, 226-239, 240, 243

DRA = Douay-Rheims
16, 27, 49, 105, 147-148, 150-153, 155-163, 165-167, 169, 174-177, 181, 184, 186-187, 189-192, 194, 196-198, 200-208, 211, 213-214, 216, 221, 224, 226-232, 234-236, 238-239, 241, 243

ERV = English Revised Version
15, 16, 33, 37, 49, 58-67, 69, 70, 72, 106-107, 121, 129, 138-177, 180-198, 200-239, 241, 242, 243

ESV = English Standard Version
16, 24, 27, 33, 37, 49, 68, 77-79, 128-129, 138-239, 241, 242, 244

GNB = Good News Bible
16, 27, 33, 37, 49, 105, 138-153, 155-218, 220-239, 241, 242, 244

GWN = God's Word to the Nations
16, 33, 37, 49, 121, 138-140, 142-143, 145-217, 219-239, 241, 242, 244

HNV = Hebrew Names Version of the WEB
16, 33, 145, 148, 151-152, 155, 158-159, 162-165, 167, 171, 175, 177-182, 186-187, 206, 209, 214, 226-227, 238-239, 241, 243, 244

ICB = International Children's Bible
16, 33, 37, 49, 138-140, 142-143, 145-153, 155-187, 189-217, 219-239, 241, 243, 244

ISV = International Standard Version
16, 37, 41, 49, 139-140, 142, 145-184, 186-196, 198, 200-209, 211-217, 219-239, 241, 243, 244

JB = Jerusalem Bible
16, 27, 33, 37, 76, 130, 138-140, 142, 145-198, 200-217, 219-239, 241, 242, 243

LB = Living Bible
16, 37, 49, 104-107, 139-140, 142-143, 145-153, 155-159, 161-180, 182-187, 189-216, 219-233, 236-238, 241, 243

MOF = The Bible, a New Translation
16, 27, 33, 37, 49, 69, 138-221, 223-239, 241, 242, 243

MRC = Messianic Renewed Covenant
16, 27, 41, 49, 138-177, 179-196, 198-218, 220-239, 241, 242, 244

MSG = The Message
16, 33, 37, 49, 114-123, 138-143, 145-153, 155-195, 197-204, 206-212, 214-218, 220-224, 226-239, 241, 242, 244

NAB = New American Bible
16, 27, 33, 37, 49, 138-143, 145-224, 226-239, 241, 242, 243

NAS = New American Standard
16, 27, 40-41, 49, 77, 80-91, 93, 102, 104, 127-128, 138-177, 179-239, 241, 242, 244

NAU = Updated NAS
16, 27, 40-41, 49, 80, 90-91, 103, 128, 138-177, 179-239, 241, 242, 244

NCV = New Century Version
16, 33, 37, 49, 138-153, 155-239, 241, 242, 244

NEB = New English Bible
16, 27, 33, 37, 49, 83, 138-140, 142-217, 219-239, 241, 242, 243

NET = New English Translation
16, 27, 33, 37, 49, 129, 138-141, 143-239, 241, 242, 244

NIrV = New International Readers Version
16, 33, 37, 49, 92, 100, 102-103, 138-141, 143-153, 155-239, 241, 242, 244

NIV = New International Version
14, 16, 33, 34-37, 49, 77, 83, 92-103, 127-128, 138-141, 143-239, 241, 242, 244

NJB = New Jerusalem Bible
16, 27, 33, 37, 49, 76, 83, 130, 138-140, 142-143, 145-206, 208-217, 219-239, 241, 243, 244

NLT = New Living Translation
16, 27, 33, 37, 49, 104, 106-107, 128, 138-140, 142-153, 155-206, 208-239, 241, 242, 244

NRS = New Revised Standard
16, 27, 33, 37, 49, 68, 69, 74-79, 89, 91, 102, 128, 138-140, 142-217, 219-239, 241, 242, 244

NWT = New World Translation
17, 33, 37, 49, 72, 76, 102, 122, 129, 138-140, 142-153, 155-177, 179-239, 241, 242, 244

Phi = New Testament in Modern English
17, 33, 37, 71, 138-143, 145-153, 155-187, 189-206, 208-217, 219-239, 241, 242, 243

REB = Revised English Bible
17, 27, 33, 37, 49, 130, 138-140, 142-198, 200-217, 219-238, 241, 242, 244

RSV = Revised Standard Version
17, 27, 33, 37, 49, 68-74, 76-78, 83, 89, 91, 102, 138-140, 142-217, 219-239, 241, 242, 243

TCW = The Clear Word
17, 49, 147-158, 160-162, 164-170, 173, 176-190, 192-199, 201-204, 206, 208, 212-216, 220-222, 228-231, 233-237, 239, 241, 243, 244

TNIV = Today's New International Version
17, 27, 33, 37, 77, 92, 99-102, 122, 128, 138-140, 142-217, 219-239, 241, 242, 244

WEB = World English Bible
16, 17, 148, 151-152, 155, 158-159, 162, 164-167, 171, 175, 177-182, 187, 206, 209, 214, 226, 238-239, 241, 243, 244

WNT = Weymouth New Testament
17, 33, 37, 49, 138-140, 142-239, 241, 242, 243

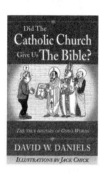
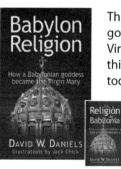

1347625 3715

ALEX